REVOLUTION
IN THE
CHURCH

SHAKING
IN THE
WORLD

by Andrew Strom

RevivalSchool

REVOLUTION IN THE CHURCH
-SHAKING IN THE WORLD

Copyright © 2023 by Andrew Strom. All rights reserved.

Permission is granted to photocopy and pass around copies of this book – so long as it is done for no charge. So yes - you can photocopy it! However, this book may not be reprinted in book form or placed on the Internet without the express permission of the author.

Published by: RevivalSchool
www.revivalschool.com

Wholesale distribution by Lightning Source, Inc.

Scripture taken from the New King James Version® , Copyright © 1982 by Thomas Nelson, Inc. Used by permission. All rights reserved. (At times the KJV is also quoted).

ISBN-13: 978-0-9831866-0-1

ISBN-10: 098318660X

1. Religion – Pentecostal   2. Religion - Revival

CONTENTS

Chapter One.
  A New Awakening 5

Chapter Two.
  Economic Shaking 21

Chapter Three.
  Revival & Reformation 31

Chapter Four.
  Shaken & Stirred 45

Chapter Five.
  Out of the Wilderness 55

Chapter Six.
  Rise of the Davids 69

Chapter Seven.
  A Media Reformation 85

Chapter Eight.
  Hallmarks of the Revolution 99

Appendix A.
  Shocking Bible Study 109

CHAPTER ONE

A NEW AWAKENING

The date is February 8, 2023. Something quite unusual has broken out at a Christian college in Kentucky – something that I believe has much deeper implications, not just for the USA, but also for the world. Here is what I wrote about it to our readers on the internet:

ASBURY REVIVAL - The DEEPER MEANING
by Andrew Strom

So what are we to make of the recent "Asbury Revival" that broke out at a Christian University in Kentucky a couple of weeks ago? Well, reports state that it started with confession of sin, deep repentance and testimonies from the students themselves (as well as heartfelt worship and prayer). This went on for many hours and word got out via Social Media. Hundreds of people began to come.

This is the kind of thing I look for in any "revival" movement. What is at the core of it? Is it repentance? Is it conviction of sin? Can we see the holiness of God at work? In my view, we can see these things clearly at Asbury - so this movement certainly has my support. (Sadly they are shutting down the public meetings soon, as they have been totally overwhelmed with visitors). I would love to see such a movement sweep through the USA and the entire Western world. God knows how much we need it!

THE DEEPER MEANING

As you may know, another famous Asbury Revival occurred on the same campus in 1970. (There are books and videos on this). I think it is important to notice the timing.

When the door first opened for me to preach in America in 2003, an astonishing thing happened that had never happened to me before. A short time before I was due to fly out, God literally gave me a sermon in my sleep - a message I had never even imagined or thought of. It was all to do with the "50-year cycle" of Awakenings in America - and what a disaster it would be if that cycle was broken.

A 50 year cycle of revivals? I had never heard of such a thing! And yet, when I went back and looked through the history books, there it was! Awakenings in America roughly every 50 years - going all the way back to the First Great Awakening of the 1740s.

When I went to America on that first trip, I found this to be one of the most anointed sermons I had ever preached. ("Thundering in Nashville" is a good example). It was basically a call to prayer - that the 'cycle' would not be broken.

And yet, when my family and I left America in 2008, after 4 years of preaching across the nation, I was very downcast - deeply concerned that my message had failed. Had the moment been lost? Was the 50-year cycle even worth talking about any more?

But I want you to look at the timing of Asbury for a moment. What was happening in America in the days of the 1970 revival? Well, it was the start of the "Jesus Movement" - a kind of 'long-haired' youth revival that produced leaders such as Keith Green, etc. It was also the "good" part of the

Charismatic movement - before the 'Prosperity' doctrine and other weird stuff entered in. Asbury in 1970 happened just as a widespread move of the Holy Spirit was sweeping through the land. And it impacted many other nations as well.

Now, roughly 50 years later in 2023 we get another Asbury. What does this speak of? Well, to me, one thing it says loud and clear is that the 50-year cycle of Awakenings in America is NOT LOST. The 'jubilee' pattern is not broken. The potential for another Awakening is still there. And to me that is a tremendous joy and relief.

But as I have said, I still believe this decade will be one of great "shaking" - and it cannot be avoided. We will have to get used to revival in the midst of judgments, a great tidal-wave of "CHANGE" in the church - and a "storm-harvest" in the fields - all occurring at once.

A window of revival is opening in America and the world - a window that only seems to open every 50 years or so. How long does it typically stay open? Perhaps 7 or 8 years, judging by history.

What does this mean for you and me? It means "pray and go forth". It means 'seize the day'. It means the wilderness is over and a new day has dawned. Spread your nets, launch into the deep. A new season is here - the exact season you and I were built for. A "window" of revival has opened - and we must not let it pass us by.

ASBURY IS A SIGN

The term 'bellwether' is defined in the dictionary as "something that indicates a trend". When I did some further research on the revivals at Asbury, this was the term that immediately came to mind. Whenever there is revival or Awakening in the air in

America, you can look to Asbury and see confirmation of it there. This pattern goes back well over 100 years.

I spoke of a "50-year cycle" in my above piece. Another way of looking at it is that God seems to send revivals in waves or clusters. Very early in the 20th Century came a giant wave centered around the Welsh Revival of 1904. Dotted all around it were revivals in Australia (1902), America (1905-06), Manchuria (1906), Korea (1907) and other places.

What was happening at Asbury University during this period? Well, they had two powerful revivals there – one in 1905 and the other in 1908. Both seemed to be centered around deep repentance, confession of sin, and prayer – much like the recent one.

Again we see the same thing 50 years later in the next giant wave. Beginning in 1947 a new cluster of revivals hit America, Canada, Argentina, the Hebrides (UK) and the Congo (Africa) – among others. So what was happening at Asbury? Another powerful revival engulfed the campus in 1950, right on time. This one became so famous that the university was front-page news across America – much like recent times.

We have already discussed the well-known revivals that hit Asbury in 1970 and 2023. One of the interesting things about the revivals at this University is that historically they have been very short and sharp – usually lasting less than three weeks each.

Hopefully by now you can see why I consider Asbury to be such a bellwether – a sign that a new "window" is opening in America and the world. It is a signal pointing to the fact that God is on the move again and the church worldwide needs to get ready. But this time it will not just be a wave of revival alone. I also believe a great wave of "change" and reformation lie directly ahead – an era unlike anything we have yet seen in the church.

MY EYES ARE OPENED

Jump back to the year 1983. I have just deeply repented and been filled with the Holy Spirit for the first time at age 17. Raised in a praying home, I discover on my dad's bookshelf a treasure-trove of books on past revivals. My heart leaps at the accounts of piercing preaching, deep conviction of sin, and great outpourings of the Holy Spirit in nation after nation. Stories of Azusa Street and the Welsh Revival fill my mind, and my heroes become men like Charles Spurgeon, John Wesley and Martin Luther.

Jump to the year 1993. I am now a writer on revivals and also editor of a newsletter called the NZ Revival Bulletin in my home nation of New Zealand. It is a small publication, but one thing this newsletter does is to bring me in touch with praying and prophetic people right across the country. And I am astonished to find that God has been speaking very similar things to a lot of these people.

What is at the heart of the prophecies and visions these people have been receiving? The words REVIVAL and CHANGE are at the very core of them. God is telling us over and over that a great shaking is ahead – and that He is going to bring a tidal wave of change to the church. The entire way that Christianity functions in the earth is going to be transformed – back to the New Testament. It is not specified when this new era might begin, but it seems these changes will occur rapidly once they get started.

As the great reformer Martin Luther said: **"Learn from me, how difficult a thing it is to throw off errors confirmed by the example of all the world, and which, through long habit, have become a second nature to us."**

Several years later in 1996 I take the NZ Revival Bulletin onto the internet for the first time. We start an email newsletter that will one day be known as the international "Revival" List and reach thousands of readers around the globe. I am now in touch with huge numbers of praying and prophetic people – not just in my own nation, but across the planet. And amazingly, many of them have been hearing the exact same things from God. A great tsunami of CHANGE lies directly ahead.

1996 is also the year that I publish my first book online – a book that is full of many of the visions and prophecies I have been talking about. It is also full of the lessons I have gleaned from past revivals. I feel led to entitle the book, **The Coming Great Reformation,** and the subtitle reads: "New Insights into the Coming Worldwide Shaking, Reformation and Street Revival".

Included in the book is one of the most inspiring quotes on revival that I have yet found:

> **"In the various crises that have occurred in the history of the church, men have come to the front who have manifested a holy recklessness that astonished their fellows. When Luther nailed his theses to the door of the cathedral at Wittemburg, cautious men were astonished at his audacity. When John Wesley ignored all church restrictions and religious propriety and preached in the fields and by-ways, men declared his reputation was ruined. So it has been in all ages... there have always been found a few who were willing to be regarded reckless for the Lord."** *(Source – F. Bartleman).*

AN UNUSUAL WORD

Jump to several years later. There is a prominent prophecy doing the rounds, stating that this new era of revival would only begin after three great Christian leaders pass on. The idea seems to be that God would continue to honor the old ways while these great leaders live, and only after they are gone could a new era dawn.

As is often the way, many years go by and this prophecy is gradually forgotten – along with many of the others that God gave during the 1990s. It is not until decades later that I suddenly have cause to remember this word when I realize that not only had the famous preacher Billy Graham died in 2018, but God's "apostle to Africa" Reinhard Bonnke had also passed away the very next year in 2019. A pretty striking coincidence. The two most prominent evangelists on earth – men who had dominated their sphere of influence for generations – both suddenly gone in the space of two years.

And not only that. In the year 2021, the pastor of the world's largest church (with a million members), David Yonggi-Cho, also passed away. Again, this was a man of tremendous influence around the globe – going back decades.

Frankly, it does not matter what you think of these leaders – whether you agree with their methods, etc. That is not the point we are making here. The stark fact is that these three most prominent Christian preachers – each of them at the very top in terms of global leadership and influence – all died within four years of one another. Just consider the implications of that for a moment – and what it might represent.

THE QUEEN IS DEAD

And still we have more to add. For we not only lost the most prominent Christian preachers from the old era. We also lost the most prominent Christian sovereign on planet earth.

Queen Elizabeth II was reportedly converted to Christ in May 1955, after inviting Billy Graham to preach to a private gathering of the royal family in Windsor. By all accounts, the queen's Christian faith meant a great deal to her. In fact, she was once reported as saying that she couldn't wait to cast her crown before Jesus – just like we read about all the kings doing in the Bible (which has to be the most profound and beautiful thing any monarch has ever said).

Queen Elizabeth had by far the longest reign of any sovereign in British history. Her era spanned 70 years – all the way from her coronation in 1952 to her death in 2022. In fact, it is remarkable how closely her era matches that of Billy Graham, who came to worldwide prominence around 1947 and remained the world's most well-known evangelist all the way to his death 71 years later in 2018.

WHAT DOES IT MEAN?

Is it possible that the old prophecy was true, and that the passing of these giants signifies the beginning of a new era in the church? Well, who can say for sure? But speaking personally, I just cannot believe it is mere coincidence that we lost the biggest pastor and the two most prominent evangelists on the planet – all within a few years of each other. The sheer timing simply screams of significance, in my view. (Especially considering Asbury in 2023).

I believe we are headed into an era that is fundamentally different from that which went before. We are leaving behind the age of the "one man band" – the one prominent leader up the front – and we are coming into an era of the whole body of Christ functioning in all it's fullness – where every Christian is seen as a "minister". The one-man concept has had its day. Full body ministry is the way of the future.

This is not to say that there will be no leaders in the coming move of God. The book of Acts had leaders – and so will we. Leadership is vitally important in any biblical revival (which is why Jesus spent three years training up His leaders for the early church). But the great difference will be the type of leadership that God will employ.

Gone are the days when the whole church sits around watching a small handful of men doing all the ministry. The one-man pastor and the one-man evangelist – these are the hallmarks of a bygone age. What is coming is a style of leadership that is more akin to a "coach" or trainer. Leaders that are passionate about releasing the whole body of Christ. Their entire focus will be on equipping the saints for the work of the ministry – raising up every Christian to become all that they are called to be.

THE CHURCH UNSHACKLED

I also believe there is to be a fundamental shift in the way Christianity is lived out. For too long the church has hidden itself away behind four walls. We have a "cathedral" mentality that has changed very little since the dark ages. In many cases our church buildings have become almost a "prison" to us – keeping our message and ministry locked away from the eyes of the world – making us inward-looking and inwardly focused.

Just like medieval times, we have our "priest" up the front doing all the work – while the laity sits in the pews. Our four walls trap us inside and keep our message from truly impacting the lost all around us. This is nothing like the early church.

Think about the ministry of Jesus for a moment. He preached and healed the sick every day – out where the people were. His ministry took place in the open, for all the world to see (and it was the same with the apostles at Solomon's Porch). This is not just a matter of being outdoors. It is the concept of visibility. It is the basic idea of a faith that presents itself out where the people are – not hiding itself away. And to do this effectively we must demonstrate the power of God.

Imagine Jesus without His miracles. Imagine the apostles without signs or healings. The gospels would not be the gospels. The book of Acts would not be the book of Acts. Miracles are not an "optional extra". They are absolutely essential if we are going to properly present Christianity to a lost and dying world. Take the power of God away and you no longer represent the message or the faith that the original apostles stood for. The gospel you are preaching is no longer a "full" gospel.

All of these aspects are going to come into crystal-clear focus as this new era of Christianity unfolds. We are entering the age of a very different church than what has been seen in the decades before. It will be far more like the New Testament. The book of Acts is coming back to life.

NOT JUST ATTENDEES

The word "discipleship" is going to be at the very heart of this new move of God. The idea of truly becoming an "imitator" of Christ. Every Christian is to be a disciple, and every disciple is to be an "apprentice" of Jesus – becoming just like Him in message, in power, and in devotion to the Father.

The current church system has taught believers to be passive – to simply sit and watch rather than being an "activist" Christian. We have gone around the world making church-goers of all nations instead ot disciples. But all that is about to change.

Think of a mechanic school for a minute. Think how practical everything is. The trainees are there to learn how to take apart engines and put them back together again. And so that is what they do. (To be sure there is a little bit of Theory as well – but even that has a practical tone to it). And if the trainees become apprenticed to a Master mechanic they will continue to learn how to take cars and engines apart – getting better and better at fixing the problem. The whole idea is to become just like the Master.

Notice how much better at "discipling" the mechanic school is than the modern church. The trainees all know what they are there for, and they are being trained up in the most practical way possible – to "learn by doing."

The church is supposed to be a training school too. It is supposed to be a place for training up disciples. That is what Jesus did for three years. And that is what the early church did. But today we are happy simply to make church-goers of everyone. People who attend buildings. People who sing songs and put money in the offering. People who are told over and over about the life of Jesus, but who actually spend very little time "imitating" Him at all. It is the very epitome of Jesus' warnings about being doers of the word, and not just hearers only.

Naturally, this is another major thing that is going to change drastically in coming years. The church is about to get back in the discipleship business in a big way. In fact, you could almost say that what is coming is a "disciple-making" revival. That is how central this concept will be to everything the church is about to become.

A SPIRITUAL RESET

Earlier we noted that the passing of those three major Christian leaders (and one Christian monarch) were all clustered around the years 2018 to 2022. What clearer sign of a "changing of the guard" and the start of a new era could there be?

But of course there is another major event that also confirms the significant timing of all this. The COVID-19 pandemic, which lasted from 2020 to 2022, was not really remarkable for its severity, but rather for the staggering decision to shut down large sectors of society for months or years on end. There is a conspiracy theory that says globalists wanted to use this as a so-called "great reset" to gain power for themselves. Well, maybe they did. But one thing I certainly believe. This entire event acted as a kind-of "spiritual reset" for the church as well – a 'great pause' before the beginning of a whole new era. (God has always known and used the ways of men for His own purposes).

How can anyone see the timing of all this as mere coincidence? First comes a mass changing of the guard at the highest levels. Then comes a three-year enforced "gap" that only serves to confirm the change in spiritual season. And now, clearly, we must conclude that a new era in the church is opening up – in which much will be shaken and transformed.

Personally, since the end of the pandemic, as I have begun to travel and minister in places like Africa and Fiji, I have seen abundant evidence of a new season and a new move of God. The word is holding sway like never before, with miracles and signs following, the like of which I have never seen.

In May 2020, near the start of the pandemic, I published a word about this change of season – and how we should respond:

REMNANT - THIS is YOUR HOUR - A Word
by Andrew Strom

Deaths, job losses, closures… We cannot downplay the tragedy of what is happening here. But I have a very different word for the Remnant of God. You know who you are.

Despite all this tragedy, to those who have been "waiting" in the caves and the rocks and the depths of the wilderness - I say, "Lift up your eyes." The very season you have been waiting for is here. Your true ministry is about to begin.

We are living in the "sudden stop." We are living in the great 'Reset'. In 100 years when they speak of this era, they will speak of this as the moment when everything changed. Like World War II, like the Great Depression - this is the hour after which nothing will ever be the same. And Remnant – this is the season you were built for.

I am speaking to those who have been set apart. You have allowed yourself to be broken. You have trained yourself for battle. You know how to preach Repentance and Conviction of sin. You have been trained in the healing of the sick and the moving of the Holy Spirit. You know how to baptize, to pray powerfully – and to train others. You are a fully-equipped preacher of the true gospel.

You have used your time well. You have paid down your debt. Your hands are free of shackles – and you're ready to go. You have a boldness and an audacity about you. While others shrink back, you will jump forward. You were built for such a time as this.

Some of you 65+ will come out of retirement. Your latter years will be much more fruitful than the former ones. The old era did not welcome you. The new era has no choice. "Fortune favors the brave," goes the saying. And this has never been more true than it is now.

While others fear – you are bold. While others play it safe – you see this hour for what it is – and you seize the moment. Those who shrink back will miss out. Those who are alert – and move forward with boldness – will have the field almost to themselves.

I say to the remnant, "Lift up your eyes." Everything has changed. Do not confine your gaze to your own nation. Many of you will be headed overseas. "But," you say, "The planes are grounded. Most nations are closed." Yes – for now that is true. But before long there will be travel again. And the people will be hungry for a word from the Lord. Especially the poor.

Where once you were ignored – now you will be welcomed. Where once you were constrained – now you will be loosed. Where once you were disregarded – now you will be respected. "Who dares wins." Go forth like Joshua and take the land.

Do not be distracted. Politics is a distraction. Current events are a distraction. Social media is a distraction. Keep your eye on the prize – the big picture. Today's harvest is whiter than it's ever been. Be alert. Watch for the doors to open and for the Lord's timing. Act with boldness. Seize the day.

Most of the world will be in turmoil. Most of the people will be shrinking back. Very few will be traveling. Many churches and businesses will be in trouble. But you will be looking around with alert eyes – for where the Lord may send you.

Do not fear. Go forth with boldness. The former things are passed away. Remnant – this is the hour you were built for. Don't let it pass you by.

As you can see from the above word, this change of season already felt very real to me even during lockdown in 2020. I was convinced that what was coming would be fundamentally different from what had gone before. For those who had been waiting upon the Lord, it would be an era of open doors and powerful ministry the like of which they had never seen.

However, there was also to be a "dark" side to this change in season. Just nine months later in February 2021 I published the word below, which was designed to be a kind-of follow-up to the previous one:

PROPHECY – A DECADE of SHAKING
by Andrew Strom

Ten years ago my family moved for a time to a little country town here in New Zealand. While I was there I met a Christian man who had shifted his entire family out of the city into this little town because he believed that "Peak Oil" and other calamities were imminent. He felt the need for a place of safety.

I told him that I believed the 2020s would be the decade when the real shaking would happen. I said I did not sense any imminent threat at the time – though of course there are always serious incidents going on. So are the 2020s really to be a decade of shaking? Yes – I believe they are.

HARVESTING IN A STORM

Years ago a friend of mine from Australia was trying to choose a name for his prophetic newsletter. "Construction Site" was one name he was considering. "Stormharvest" was another. Immediately when he shared this I told him that "Stormharvest" had to be the one. For there is no doubt that in these last days, many of us are going to be bringing in the harvest in the midst of a giant tempest. But never fear. One can actually get used to "storm-harvesting". And that is exactly what a lot of us will be doing. We will live in the eye of the hurricane, calmly bringing in the harvest while panic is all around.

Stockmarkets may crash, oil markets may roar, divisions and schisms may roil the politics of nations – but we have a job to do – bringing in the sheaves. And brothers and sisters, our destiny is to get that job done. We need to keep our focus straight and our heart at peace. We are laborers in the harvest of the Lord – and our task is clear.

SHAKING OF THE CHURCH

The very first book I wrote back in 1996 was called "The Coming Great Reformation." I believe that book begins in this decade. Along with great shaking among the nations will come a great tidal wave of change in the church. This will not come from current church leadership. It will be forced on them from outside the ranks. The entire meaning of Christianity is going to change – back to the book of Acts. The "clergy-laity" divide will disappear and all will become "ministers". It will be the greatest revolution in the understanding of "church" since the days of Luther. Much of the existing system will be dissolved as true New Testament Christianity returns.

My friends, we are headed into a decade of shaking unlike anything that most of us have ever seen. But it is a time to be excited – not to fear or become anxious. For those with boldness, this will be a decade of great opportunity and advancement in the kingdom. Do not be among those who shrink back or hide away. Embrace the shaking, embrace the turmoil – and get to work. A lot of it will just be "noise" – more fearful in people's minds than in actual reality. Let others cower in fear. You can be one who goes forth in boldness at such a time – following the hand of the Lord.

We are living in the most momentous of times. Do not waste this window, my friends. It is time to put your boots on and get ready for a true "storm-harvest".

Today, just like always, we see postings every day on the internet by Christians who are stoking fears over what is happening in the world – causing many to shrink back in alarm. And many will indeed hide away in their basement, fearing to go forth in such stormy times. But Jesus didn't promise us a rose garden. In fact, as stated above, today's harvest can only be brought in by those who are prepared to reap in chaotic conditions. And what a great hour awaits such ones – for the fields are indeed whiter than ever – especially in the poorer nations where fewer and fewer will dare to go. The harvest is ripe beyond words – yet the laborers are so few.

Will you be such a "storm-harvester," my friend? Will you be one who dares all for Christ – to bring in such a mighty harvest? Look up, for the season has changed. Remnant, this is indeed your hour. The fields are ripe, the time is short, and the "Lord has need of thee".

CHAPTER TWO

ECONOMIC SHAKING

Speaking personally, I love the United States and have many friends in that nation. We lived there for four years and I have nephews and relatives who are Americans. But for reasons we will get into, I believe that America (and much of the Western world) has actually been under a form of economic judgment since the early 2000s.

What is the reason? Simply for the fact that the USA is a leader in the earth. In fact, she is by far the most dominant leading nation on the planet. American TV, American music, American culture and American morality have swept the globe and dominated the minds of the youth for generations. And as Jesus Himself said, "To whom much is given, much is expected". We know from Scripture that leaders are faced with a stricter judgment. And as the media juggernaut of the planet, the USA has to take some responsibility for the spiritual and moral wasteland that her media have created around the world.

You cannot get away forever with calling yourself a "Christian" nation and yet being the moral and spiritual cesspool of the earth. America is the leader, and God will not take it lightly when such a nation – founded on Christian principles – becomes a force for such depravity across the globe.

When I lived and ministered in the States from 2004 to 2008, I used to warn my audiences of these things over and over. In particular I warned of steadily increasing economic judgments – especially in the years leading up to the Great Recession of 2008.

(Of course, I was not alone in this. Other preachers like David Wilkerson had been issuing similar warnings for years).

TIME TO GET OUT

In the early months of 2008 I felt led to take my family and leave the United States for our home nation of New Zealand. I left with a heavy heart, believing that my message of repentance and my warnings of judgment had not been truly received.

Just months later in September 2008 came the very crash that we had been warning about. The two largest mortgage giants in the world (Fannie Mae & Freddie Mac) failed, the largest insurance company on earth and the largest thrift bank in the USA both collapsed, Lehman Brothers went bankrupt (almost taking the entire financial system with it), money markets reeled, the investment banking industry crumbled, and the stock market suffered its worst-ever one-day loss, plunging 777 points in a single day. The Great Recession had begun.

Of course, the Federal Reserve and the US government did what they have always done in recent times. They flooded the system with easy money – not caring if they created another "bubble" in the process. This artificial prop-up job has become the go-to method that Central Banks use when the markets catch a cold. They used it in the late 1990s with the Dotcom bubble. They used it in the mid-2000s with the Housing bubble. And now they have used it again during the 2010s – thus creating an "Everything" bubble of gigantic proportions.

But you cannot get away with such bubble-blowing excess forever. Each time requires more and more froth being pumped into the system. Eventually the last bubble will burst and the entire house of cards is liable to come crashing down.

As we saw in the last chapter, I published a warning in 2021 that the decade of the 2020s is to be one of tremendous shaking. I am convinced that a large part of this will be financial and economic in nature. Of course, we can expect political and military shaking of an exceptional kind as well (like the war in Ukraine that started the following year).

The United States itself is about as divided and angry today as it has ever been, and it would not surprise me at all to see actual civil conflict on the streets. (There are prophecies of this). My only hope is that a kind-of brokenness and humility will come about through all this turmoil, that widespread revival might result. A proud and wayward nation needs a season of "breaking" in order to prepare her heart.

I am convinced that God has indeed been preparing an army for this time. Hidden in the silent pews, in the caves and wildernesses, disillusioned with "church as we know it", longing and crying and praying for something more – some of them have been in training for years. Others are the youth who will make up a significant part of God's mighty army in these last days. What we are looking at is a great Reformation, a street revival, a youth revival, and a great harvest – all rolled into one. And all occurring in the midst of some of the darkest days that the West has ever known.

PORTENTS OF A COLLAPSE

As we have seen, a lot of the old forgotten prophecies from the 1990s are now coming into sharper focus. Some are at least 30 years old. But it is also interesting to look back at the words we published in the years 2006 to 2008, warning of an imminent economic crash in the United States. I believe many of these warnings are just as applicable today – maybe even more so. (And of course they apply much more widely than just to the USA – which is where I was living at the time). Here are some examples, so you can see what I mean:

"AMERICA IN THE BALANCES" – 14 Dec 2006
by Andrew Strom

Complacency. Apathy. -These are the greatest downfalls of the 'lukewarm' church. "We are increased with goods, and have need of nothing," as the Scripture so rightly says.

So what does God do with a country like America today? -A country that has historically been a "Land of Revivals" but is now addicted to "consumerism" en masse. A country that for the first time since the Great Depression now has a negative savings rate - because its people are so enamored with owning "things" - even if they can't afford them. A country whose people are indebted to their eyeballs and beyond - so they can keep up the lifestyle of ease to which they have grown accustomed.

What does God do with an America that has grown too fat to pray? Is anybody "desperate" any more? Where are those who cry to God from their gut - from the bottom of their heart? Where are the agonies and tears? Has America forgotten what kind of prayer it takes to obtain an Awakening? If we can't pray like that any more, then surely all is lost?

But just how 'desperate' are things really, you ask? Things aren't so terrible, surely?

Well, the fact is that this nation's sin right now is utterly unmatched in her entire history. Has there ever been a generation of Americans that has killed 40 million babies in just 30 years? No, such a thing is unprecedented. And has there ever been an American generation that has not only celebrated homosexuality - but actually helped broadcast and spread it around the earth? No, such a thing has never been seen before. Forty years ago it would have been undreamt-of.

(-God reserves for these particular types of sin the term, "abominations" - and historically any nation practicing them has been utterly destroyed).

Has there ever been an American generation that has addicted the whole earth to soft porn and violence the way that Hollywood has done in the last 40 years? No, again this is unprecedented in history. (The center of the worldwide pornography industry is located just outside Los Angeles).

Has there ever been an American generation whose preachers go on satellite television and teach other leaders in 'Revival' countries how to "milk" the sheep for money, and grow rich at the expense of the poor? No, I tell you, America has never done this before. Our TV preachers are now actually being used by the devil to corrupt true moves of God all over the globe. (Go to Nigeria, Ghana, Brazil and see what I mean. American "Prosperity" is everywhere - and still spreading).

At this very moment America is hanging in the balances. God is making up His mind what to do with her. And yet still complacency rules. -Still no "desperate" prayer. Apathy covers us like a blanket. Will you sleepwalk your way to destruction, America?

Years ago a famous preacher commented that if God did not judge America, then He would have to apologize to Sodom and Gomorrah. I am not sure that it was true then, but I certainly believe it is true now. We are at the crisis point. In the last 40 years, in every way we have become the most sick, selfish, greedy, corrupt, sin-addicted generation that America has ever produced. And now judgment hangs over the land like a sword.

Where are those who "sigh and cry" at the abominations in the land? Where are those like righteous Lot whose soul was "tortured" day after day by all that he saw and heard? Are there none who will cry to God with strong weeping and tears?

Let me make some predictions at this point, so I can be clear about what this country is facing:

(1) Firstly, I believe it is impossible to avoid judgment. This nation may have revival in the midst of judgments - but this is now the best it can hope for. In fact, without judgments it is doubtful that revival is even possible. -People are simply too complacent. They need a shock even to begin to pray.

(2) Expect a great economic crash - and expect it soon. Without this, how will this nation get its eyes off its great god, Money?

(3) Expect further calamity. This nation is "running red lights" one after the other. -That is what 9-11 and Katrina were. Things are going to get much much worse before this is over. Expect something to hit the West Coast - and expect it to be bad.

It is difficult for me to put into words the crisis we are in at this moment, and the judgments that await this nation if there is no repentance. God is looking for sackcloth and ashes. He is looking for those who "sigh and cry". Will you be one of these, my friend? The hour is late. The need is urgent. Who will respond?

"HAS THE CRASH BEGUN??" - March 14, 2007
by Andrew Strom

I remember very vividly kneeling down by my bed soon after the towers fell on 9-11 and hearing God clearly speak to me- "The HORNS of AMERICAN FINANCIAL POWER HAVE FALLEN, HAVE FALLEN." To me this was a profound and shocking word, which I published that same week.

I felt strongly that in following years we would see this play out before our eyes. -The unraveling of US financial power in the earth. (I was made to understand it was like the Titanic - which hit the iceberg but did not sink for many hours. In a lot of ways, the sinking of that vessel was symbolic of Britain's decline as a world power from that point on. -I know this is shocking to contemplate regarding the US. -It certainly shocked me at the time).

After 9-11, I continued to publish occasional articles about a coming economic crash. Meanwhile an enormous Housing bubble was building in America.

Eight months ago we began to publish warnings about the bursting of this Housing bubble, and the likely impact it would have - beginning in 2007. ("WORST HOUSING SLUMP in 50 YEARS?" - published Aug 30, 2006).

I began to refer to this coming financial judgment in my sermons, saying that in many ways it would be God's mercy - to shock us out of our complacency and apathy - and to cause us to desperately seek His face. We have allowed comfort and materialism to turn our heads. We have become lazy - "lovers of pleasures more than lovers of God". Only by striking this country's great idol 'Mammon' can God cause us to cry out to Him. We have no idea how lukewarm we have become...

For some time I have wondered what it will take to get us really praying in this nation. What calamity will need to occur? Do we really need a full-blown crisis staring us in the face before we will go to our knees? -Perhaps we do.

"STOCK MARKETS SLUMPING - WHY??" - Jul 27, 2007
by Andrew Strom

... I was crying out to God about all this yesterday, and one thing I was strongly led to pray was that this economic crisis will not be "wasted" on us. In other words, as things grow worse, that this nation will not harden its heart at losing its precious "lifestyle", but rather that its heart will be softened and broken - and become hungry for spiritual things once again. -That the complacency and apathy that comes with materialism will be broken - and people will begin to seek God more and more with all their heart. -That this crisis not be wasted on us - but that great good might come of it.

For there are two main paths that nations can take when major crises hit - and affect their lifestyle and standard of living. -They can either grow hardened and bitter against God, or they can become more broken and softened and hungry towards Him. We need to pray that the latter will be the case. In fact, we need to be urgent in prayer that this crisis will not be "wasted" on the Western nations, but that it will prepare our lands for revival - that it will help to "break up the fallow ground".

As I said, this could go either way, my friends. We really do need to pray that our nations will not become hardened, but rather humble and broken and spiritually hungry through what is happening.

"THE DREADED "D" WORD" - Nov 8, 2007
by Andrew Strom

Carter Conlon says that he was in a poor African nation recently where there are 700,000 little children living without parents on the streets - and yet the pastors are driving BMW's and preaching selfish Prosperity. Where did they get such sickness? -They got it from America. We beam it to them live by satellite.

And this is why I believe God is about to make an EXAMPLE of the USA. -He has to. All the nations follow her lead. The entire church worldwide looks to her for guidance. And she has become a center of corruption and spiritual sickness almost without precedent in the history of the world. She has made the whole earth "drunk" with her fornications, her movies, her MTV, her music, her rebellion, her love of money. And so I am convinced that God is about to make an 'example' of her before all nations. He cannot have a "Christian" country spreading such things in the earth.

When I am in Nigeria again this February I plan to preach this very thing. -That God is making an example of America so that all the nations will fear. -That this is what happens when you follow a creed of "God wants me rich", of pleasure-seeking, materialism, selfishness and greed. -That God is about to demonstrate to the whole earth what will happen to such a nation. Do you think He is just going to stand by and watch us ruin His revivals forever?

"HOW TO SURVIVE THE DEPRESSION" - Jan 31, 2008
by Andrew Strom

I remember one place that I preached in 2006, predicting that there would be a housing crash followed by an economic depression. There was a man smirking and laughing down the back of the room. I guess that smirk may be missing now...

There is only one type of Christian that I believe will survive – and maybe even thrive – during the coming Depression - and that is the Christian who is ministering actively to the poor. It does not matter how much gold or US T-bills you store up. It is only "heavenly treasure" that will do. Do not expect to do well if you only selfishly consider yourself and your own family. Those who are ministering to the poor and needy I believe have a chance to literally thrive in this situation, while those who "hoard to themselves" can expect God's great displeasure. He is simply not going to put up with it any more.

I guess one of the questions that arises is whether the Great Recession of 2008–2009 qualifies as a "depression" or not. Certainly it is seen by economists as the worst financial crisis since the Great Depression. But like the slump of the 1930s, which came in two phases (1929 and 1937), I have always believed this one has yet to expend its full force. The authorities stepped in and spent trillions on a giant prop-up job that I believe will ultimately fail. It will be very interesting to see what the 2020s bring.

MONEY-CHANGERS

One of the most important points made above is that this is not just a judgment on the values and lifestyle of the West, but more importantly on the values and lifestyle of the church.

The Bible states that judgment begins at the house of God, and we need to realize that God is going to use this crisis to root worldliness and the love of money out of His church. He is going to separate the gospel of ease and Mammon from his pure and undefiled gospel. He is going to drive the money-changers out of the temple. That is what a lot of this shaking is about.

As we have seen, this "gain is godliness" gospel has infiltrated many nations around the globe. The American mega-church syndrome is alive and well even in the Third World – and certainly throughout the West. A lot of it is about money, success, "giving to get", tithing, hype and selfishness. It is the very opposite of "taking up the cross" – the very opposite of "Blessed are the poor in spirit." Basically it is the total opposite of everything Jesus stood for. And He is about to use this crisis to drive it into the sea – along with all who preach it. Jesus wants His church back!

CHAPTER THREE

REVIVAL & REFORMATION

I hope after reading the above, that you can see why it makes so much sense that God would use an era of global crisis to purge and cleanse His wayward church – and prepare the nations for revival. Great shaking and great Reformation truly do go hand in hand. And thus we can expect an era of unprecedented change and turmoil directly ahead.

The truth is, God is sick and tired of man running the church in his own way – with the arm of the flesh. God wants the reins back! And He is going to take them back whether we like it or not. Below is an insightful vision given to a preacher in the 1970s that relates to this very thing:

VISION OF THE SWORD & THE SERPENT
by L, Vere Elliot

This is the vision/revelation: I was in the midst of a great meeting hall (a church), and the walls and ceilings were covered with jewels and ornaments, and the windows were made of colored glass (a typical cathedral or church). The hall was full of people, some rich, some poor, some sick and crippled, mute and blind; but all had chains on and were handcuffed, and no one was free (a picture of today's church, they're in church but they're not free).

In front of the meeting hall was a large platform, with a pulpit on one side and a large cage on the other, with a huge green serpent in it; and hanging over where the speaker would stand, was a great sword suspended by two strings horizontally; and on the platform were several ministers, 8 or 10, clothed in clerical robes, sitting one behind the other, one seated just a little above the other.

The assembly looked upon these men and they looked upon the church. There was silence for a while, until a thundering voice sounded from the pulpit, as if it came directly from God, saying, Who will declare the whole counsel of God? And the first clergyman arose with a Bible in his hand, and when he did, the old green serpent uncoiled and stretched out hissing against the man with sparkling eyes and protruding fangs; and the man of God, falsely so-called, sank back into his seat and placed his Bible under the chair. And when the serpent stretched up his head and touched the sword, he said to that man, "Anyone who obeys the voice of God, I will kill with this sword." And for a little while, there was silence again.

And then the Voice sounded from the pulpit again, "Who will declare the whole counsel of God?" And then the second man in clerical robes arose as if he would step forward, and again the serpent uncoiled against him, and he tumbled back with fear and sat down and placed his Bible under his chair (hiding the Word). The serpent again touched the sword, and with the same remark said, "I will kill you, if you obey the voice of God."

And for the third time the Voice from the pulpit thundered, and a third man arose and sat down like the two before him. And again and again the Voice sounded until each of the clergymen had had an opportunity to resist the serpent, but fear overcame them all, like the first three had been overcome. And the serpent smiled with his evil smile. And then the Voice sounded again from the pulpit saying, "Oh if there were a man, Oh if there were a man; Oh if there were a man who would declare the whole counsel of God, that these chained men might be set free! Is there not one man?"

Then a man of little stature (meaning he was nothing in the sight of the world), ascended the platform and stood under the sword, and he lifted up his eyes toward heaven and said, "Into Thy hands, O God, I commit my spirit." Then he opened the Bible and read. He didn't add anything to it, and he didn't take anything from It; he read the Word, and spoke as a man having authority. And when he had finished, the old serpent stretched up to the edge of the sword and cut off one of the strings holding the sword in place, and the sword swung down and missed him and passed over his head; because he was a man of "little stature"; and the weight of the sword made the other string to break, and the sword swung back and pierced the hearts of those clergymen who were lined up and nailed them to the wall. And a great scream of despair sounded from the pulpit; but an even greater cry of joy sounded from the assembly, for every man's chains were loosed and they were set free! (By the word they were set free).

When this vision had vanished, I saw another vision of the Savior in a cloud, just above my head. He spoke saying, "Hear my son the meaning of these things. The meeting hall which you saw is the secularized church, having a form of godliness, but denying the power thereof. They are all covered with the jewels of the joys of this world, and there is no end to their silver and gold. The people, which you saw, are those for whom I died, but My people are destroyed for lack of knowledge; they have eyes, but they do not see; they have ears, but they cannot hear. They are truly in bondage and must be set free!"

"The platform in which you saw, on which the clergymen were sitting: The platform is the preconceived ideas, having their origins from the pit of hell. The pulpit is the throne of God; and the serpent, old Lucifer himself. The sword which you saw is the Word of God; and the strings on which it was hanging, mean the power of the Word to give life or the power of the Word to take life. Life was given to the man of little stature and life taken from the clergymen that did not preach My Word! The clergymen that you saw, are men (& women) from every church who pretend to know Me, but they teach My people things which are not written in the Book of life; and their pride and their presumption, and their worldly spirit force them to obey Satan, who is a liar and the father of lies; and each of the clergymen try and exceed the other in elegance, in extensive writings, argumentation and the like; but they only consider the" letter" of the Word, and leave out the "spirit" of the Word. And the day will come and now is at hand, when they shall all perish, just like these."

After having considered this horrible scene, the Lord spoke again with these words, "Do you remember My words in the prophecy of Jeremiah chapter 23, as well as My words in the prophecy of Ezekiel chapter 34?" Jesus said, Read it. And I opened my Bible and read, "Woe unto the shepherds that destroy and scatter the sheep of My pasture, saith the LORD" (Jer.23:1). "In the prophets I have seen a horrible thing, they commit adultery and they walk in falsehood: (a perversion of the Word of God), and strengthen the hands of evil doers" (Jer.23:14).

Jesus said, "At the end of days you shall understand this. Woe to the shepherds that feed themselves, should not the shepherds feed the flock!" (Ezek.34:2). "The weak you have not strengthened, nor have you healed the sick, you've not bound up that which was broken, and neither have you sought that which was lost; but with harshness and with rigor have you ruled over them" (Ezek.34:4). "I will destroy the fat and the strong shepherds; and I will feed them with judgment" (Ezek.34:16). Then He said to me, "That these false shepherds shall in no wise escape when the sword falls upon them. But My sheep must be warned, they must be set free!" And again

He said, "Do you remember My words in the prophecy of Jeremiah in the latter part of chapter 25? Read it!" And I read these words, "And the slain if the LORD shall be in that day from one end of the earth, even to the other end of the earth" (Jer.25:33). "Howl ye shepherds, for the day of your slaughter is come!" (Jer.25:34).

Then He said to me, "These days shall come quickly, the shepherds shall howl, yea, there shall be weeping and gnashing of teeth; but when the sword has fallen it will be too late forever. The man whom you saw who was of little stature, is every man and woman who will humble himself or herself, and be obedient even to the death of the cross, putting his or her trust in God, and going forward declaring the whole counsel of God! Oh, if I could find such a man, can you tell Me where there is one? With such a man I could shake heaven and earth, saith the LORD."

What a powerful vision! And how strikingly it reminds us of the great responsibility that every preacher has to fully speak the word of the Lord – holding nothing back. Down through history, it has only been when God has found such preachers that revival has truly come.

The sad fact is that there is so much that is unbiblical and lukewarm about our Christianity today, that it is hard to know where to start. I once did a study of the early church in the book of Acts and found that there was basically not one similarity between the way the original church was set up and ours today. Not one! The things we preach are totally different, our lack of power and authority is totally different, our understanding of "church life" is totally different, our values and lifestyles are totally different, the type of people we focus on are totally different – in fact, just about everything we do is utterly and completely different from the Bible. And in many ways it is the opposite!

SO MUCH IS LOST

Despite the thousands in our megachurches today, soaking up the warm entertainment offered to them every week, I want to put it to you that we have lost Christianity. Despite the Christian books now found in our supermarkets, and the "crossover" of Christian artists into the mainstream, and our Christian megastores and DVDs and Study-Bibles, I want to put it to you that we have lost Christianity.

Despite our lavish cathedrals in the suburbs (Charismatic or not) with their pastel hues and comfortable pews, their projector screens and $40,000 sound systems, I want to put it to you that we have utterly lost Christianity.

We left it behind somewhere when we shifted our churches from the inner city into the comfortable suburbs. We left it behind when we stopped welcoming the addicts off the street into our meetings and started welcoming only the "respectable" people. We left it behind when we stopped preaching "take up your cross" and turned the gospel into a success formula – 'Seven Steps to your Best Life Now.'

Somewhere in our comfortable suburban streetscape with its manicured lawns we lost the real thing. Somehow in our concern for "property values" and a better retirement plan we left it behind. But that is not the worst part of it. The worst part is that we don't know how to get it back again. Or perhaps we don't really WANT to get it back again. The cost simply doesn't bear thinking about, does it?

And so, as we drive around in our nice shiny cars with our new electronic toys, and attend "church" as we know it twice a week for 2 hours; As we live a life that is about as unlike Jesus as you can get, a life of comfort and coddling undreamt of by billions around the world – a lifestyle in the top 10% of the earth today (in debt up to our eyeballs all the while) – the fact is that we don't really

CARE that we have lost original Christianity, do we? We are too busy, man. Don't bother us with that kind of talk.

It will all be OK, the preacher tells us. We will all make it to heaven in the end. We are all decent people here. We have "prayed the little prayer". We have given our hearts to the Lord.

But what is this? What is that thundering voice I hear? "DEPART FROM ME." 'But Lord... But Lord....'

OUR GOSPEL - THE WORST LOSS OF ALL

When I think about the state of today's church, and the things that have the greatest impact on our Christianity today, I keep coming back to the fact that we have very largely lost the gospel. The truth is, in any era, the gospel that we preach makes all the difference in the world. In studying revival history for so many years, I want to tell you that the Great Reformation and many of the world's greatest revivals down the centuries have often been based on this one thing: Recovering the TRUE GOSPEL and preaching it with apostolic anointing and authority. But the fact is that today most of us don't even realize we have lost it!

Surely there is no tragedy in the world worse than this – the church losing the gospel. We could have a hundred terrorist attacks, or earthquakes or hurricanes, and it would still not outweigh the tragedy of this one thing – WE HAVE LOST THE GOSPEL. Nothing can compare to this disaster – nothing.

For when you lose the gospel, you lose salvation. People are actually no longer becoming saved. (Remember, Paul said that the gospel is the "power of God unto salvation"). And when people are no longer truly becoming saved, you also lose the church. For no true gospel = no true church.

People will tell me that I am being too drastic. Well, I want to say to you that I am not being drastic enough. In fact, if I were to shout through 1000 megaphones directly into your ears, it would not be possible for me to overemphasize just how disastrous and awful and horrific it is that our backslidden Western church today has – to all intents and purposes – lost its gospel. And in doing so it has lost its very reason for being.

Today we tell everybody that all they need to do is say a little rote prayer accepting Jesus as their "personal savior". Tell me, does such a thing even come close to existing in Scripture? Can you recall anyone in Acts ever saying, "Just repeat this little prayer after me"? Or "Quietly slip up your hand – no need for anyone to see"?

No, you can't. That is because nobody ever did. It is all a modern fabrication – a complete invention. This is no salvation at all. We act like people can safely forget about conviction of sin and deep repentance and water-baptism and getting filled with the Holy Spirit. Just "optional extras", eh? But look at Acts and tell me – was there ever such a thing as real Christianity without these things?

And what about getting a clean conscience (washed in the blood) and keeping it clean? Are we ever told how to walk in that today? To actually "walk" in the washing of the blood of Jesus? To be clean on the inside, to be utterly 'Clean', to be EVERY WHIT CLEAN? (The most important thing in the world). Where is this in our gospel? Where is the transformed life? Where is the freedom from sin?

We have lost it all. Our people very rarely repent. They often go for years without baptism (meaning, according to Romans 6, that their "old man" is not yet dead – and so they simply cannot live a new life in Christ). Read Romans 6 sometime and ask yourself this question- "If I have not been baptized, then is my old life "buried" with Christ or not? Is my 'old man' dead or not?" This is why the apostles always baptized people immediately.

And then we often fail to get people filled with the Spirit right away too – let alone "walking" in the Spirit. Tell me, how are we supposed to have holiness if we have not even been filled with the "Holy" Spirit? Why do you think the apostles always made sure that people became Spirit-filled right away?

Most of us do not even have "day one" Christianity as it was in the Bible. We have lost the gospel and we don't even know it. We have invented a gospel of 'convenience', a gospel without the cross, a gospel without holiness or the power to live a Christian life. A gospel that shows no-one how to get a clean conscience or how to walk in it. I want to say to you that such a gospel is no gospel at all. And we should be ashamed of ourselves for preaching such a travesty.

No wonder today's church is lukewarm! The gospel is the building block upon which everything else is built. Without it we have nothing – literally nothing. It affects all that we do and all that we are. To lose it is simply the worst disaster imaginable. So how on earth can we get it back?

Well, we have spoken about Revival many times in this book. And we need to realize that the RETURN OF THE GOSPEL was often the key that brought about these Great Awakenings of the past – the gospel being restored and preached in power. The longest-lasting revivals always involved the return of the gospel. That is precisely what was happening with the preaching of Wesley, Finney, Whitefield, etc. And it has to happen again today!

So revival to me is far more than just a fleeting visitation. It is to be the long-lasting restoration of the true gospel – and thus the true church also. If we want original Christianity restored today, we must first see the gospel restored. It is the most important key to it all. Oh God, send such a revival! Bring back the full gospel and those who will preach it! Those "mighty men and women of valor" – prepared and trained for years for a time such as this. Oh God, don't leave us the way we are!

A PICTURE OF 'ACTS'-TYPE CHRISTIANITY

To give a positive picture of the kind of Christianity I am talking about, I want you to forget about today's church for a moment – with all her apparent problems and contradictions. Imagine that you are still living in the same city, in the same year, but you are right in the middle of a 'book of Acts'-type scenario. Somehow everything has changed.

For some reason, all of the Spirit-filled Christians in your city have left their denominations and divisions behind. They are now committed to the true gospel and true Christianity. And they have begun to fulfill the prayer of Jesus - "That they all may be one". They now hold huge gatherings all over the city – right out in the open. And as well as these united gatherings, on most streets there is now a house-meeting, where all the Spirit-filled believers from each street gather together, eating and sharing and having communion, etc. The power of God flowing in these meetings is amazing. Many healings and miracles are happening all over the city.

It seems also that the church buildings and cathedrals have simply been abandoned. No longer do Christians want to hide themselves away behind "four walls". They want to gather out where the people are – presenting Jesus to the whole world. They want to be truly "one body". There is no way that any of their old buildings could contain the crowds, anyhow.

And the men whom God has raised up to lead this vast movement do not seem much like the 'Reverends' or even the televangelists of old. In fact, quite a few of them have never been to Bible College and they seem to be very plain, ordinary people from humble backgrounds. But what an anointing! It is very clear to everyone that these 'apostles and prophets' (as they are known) have spent many years in prayer and brokenness before God – drawing closer and closer to Him. When they speak, the very fear of the Lord seems to come down, and many people repent deeply of their sins. People are coming into a "clean conscience" type of Christianity – and walking in it! Demons are cast out and the blind and crippled are made whole. These kinds of things are happening all the time. The whole city is just in awe of what is going on, and thousands upon thousands are being saved. Even the newspapers and television are full of it.

As soon as someone repents they are immediately baptized in water and hands are laid on them for the infilling of the Holy Spirit. This is expected from day one. And it is also expected that every Christian has a gift and a calling from God – and that they should be encouraged to move forward and fulfill their calling. No longer is there a distinction made between those who are "ministers" and those who are merely 'laity'. Now it is expected that EVERYONE is a minister of the Lord. (However, there are 'elders' – i.e., older Christians to guide things).

Some of the bishops and pastors from several denominations have actually denounced this great move of God very strongly. They say it is "deception" and warn their people to stay away. (Every revival in history has been accused of this – usually by religious leaders). In fact the persecution is getting worse. But to be honest, it is so obvious to most people that God is the one behind it all, that very few take the opposition seriously. The Spirit of God is sweeping all before Him. The glory of the Lord has come.

One of the reasons that these leaders are so upset is that a lot of the Christians' giving now does not go to church buildings, but rather to the poor. In fact, God has spoken to many people to start supporting widows and orphans overseas, etc. They also minister to the poor of their own city and give generously to anyone in their midst who is in need. Some even sell their possessions in order to do this.

The huge overriding theme of this great movement is Love. "Behold how they love one another" is the catch-cry of many who watch this 'new church' in action. And everyone is given to much prayer.

And so, gathering "as one" in the outdoors (sometimes in arenas if the weather is bad) and breaking bread from house to house, they eat together with glad and sincere hearts, praising God and enjoying the favor of all the people. And the Lord adds to their number daily those who are being saved.

THE REAL THING

The above description is taken straight out of the Book of Acts – as applied to today. Everything in the above paragraphs is put there to give you an idea of what it would be like to live in the Jerusalem church at the start of Acts. And it was like that for years. Imagine the impact of such a church on the world around it! God is wanting to do this again. And He wants to use ordinary people like you and me to help bring it to pass.

I am convinced that we are not supposed to treat the early church as a special case. It was given as an example to us. It is what the "normal" church should be like all the time! And yet we have fallen so far below this standard. Only in times of revival do we approach it again for a period. But I believe it is supposed to be "normal" for the church to be like this – day in and day out. This is the way that Jesus always wanted us to be.

Even in Spirit-filled circles a lot of traditions are simply taken for granted in the church today that are found nowhere in the Bible. And they are blocking us from coming into the kind of Christianity described above. Preachers may fight to keep them – and probably will. But many of these leaders know deep down that a lot of this stuff is simply the 'traditions of men'. Isn't it true that we have to get rid of a bunch of these things if we are to once again live like the early church?

I am hoping that this book will make people hungry for a different kind of Christianity – the kind that was actually invented by Jesus and the apostles. And I hope that people will understand that it is not just outward structural changes that are needed, but inward 'heart' changes as well. In fact it is the heart things that must come first, otherwise nothing of value will ever be accomplished.

So what about you, my friend? Are you willing to do whatever it takes to see God restore such a glorious Christianity to the earth? Are you willing to go through tremendous shaking and change in your own life to see such a thing come about? God's eyes are roaming the earth right now for such ones that He can use. I pray that when His eyes alight upon you and I, they will not be disappointed. All that He requires is a willing heart. I pray that every one of us may be found willing in these vital days.

CHAPTER FOUR

SHAKEN & STIRRED

At the very center of the shaking that lies ahead is the Biblical principle – "The kingdom shall be taken from you and given to another." Remember, the prophet Samuel essentially spoke this to king Saul before God stripped him of the leadership of Israel and gave it to David. (1 Sa 15:22-23, 1 Sa 28:17). Jesus also spoke this to the elders and chief priests in His own day – for exactly the same reason: "The kingdom of God shall be taken from you, and given to a nation bringing forth the fruits thereof" (Mt 21:43). Their leadership role was being stripped away because they had been found unworthy – and their place was to be given to others.

This has always been at the heart of every true reformation. There has to be a total revolution in the leadership for a new era to begin. But notice that King David had to spend years being crushed and broken in the wilderness before he could be trusted to lead Israel. And this is true in our own day also.

Looking at the history of the church, such reformations (and their leaders) are often most unwelcome. For they are never "quiet, retiring" men or movements, and everything they stand for often amounts to one giant rebuke for the church. Was Luther welcomed, or Wesley, or Booth? Hardly! In fact, they were some of the most controversial figures of their day. Like Israel with her prophets, the church has rarely greeted reformers or revivalists with open arms. In fact, it has often been the existing church leaders who have persecuted new moves of God the worst.

What we need is a total revolution – back to true New Testament Christianity. But sadly it has often been found that the existing leaders are simply too invested in the status quo. And thus most true revivals and reformations usually start as "outsider" movements.

In the coming move of God, I believe this change will be seen even in the order of nations. Do not expect the leading countries to be the same as the past. Reformations by their very nature involve a change of order. And true revivals tend to be born in a "stable" rather than a palace. Expect the coming reformation to be birthed among the lowly and despised, rather than the rich and powerful.

At first people may look askance at the whole thing for this very reason. "What good thing can come out of Nazareth?" But the moving of God will be obvious to those who have eyes to see.

One of the most powerful visions that I have ever come across related to all this was given to a Christian lawyer from India named Swarna Jha – a woman who has received many stunning visions and prophecies. This one was given to her way back in 2006:

VISION: JUST ONE ROAR OF THE LION
by Swarna Jha

I saw this vision on the 22nd of August 2006.

I saw a Lion. I walked with Him to a very high Rock. The Lion then climbed the Rock, and Stood on the very top of this high Rock. I stood below, looking up at Him.

He let out a LOUD ROAR.

And EVERYTHING in the atmosphere / universe changed.

In a flash I had a 360 degree vision, and what I am about to relate happened in a flash, but I spent the whole of the 22nd of August, just waiting on God, to see in 'slow motion', what I had seen in a speedy flash, and understand what I had seen.

I was told that my mind could not grasp the vastness of the changes I saw in the Vision. So I stayed at home, and did not take up any duties but spent the whole day, off and on, every few hours just re-visiting this vision and seeing it unfurl in more detail, now at a speed that I could cope with. I don't think I have ever seen such a lengthy vision, condensed into a 360-degree vision flash before.

Frame by frame this is what I saw:

I saw Empires fall, and wars begin.

I saw that where previously, formulas and general understanding were proven, it did not work any more, where there were people and places overflowing with money one moment, the next morning the moneyed had nothing.

I saw many 'proven' thoughts, and ways now nullified.

I saw that the balance was tipped in favor of the East.

I saw Angels who had been working in the North and Northwest, recalled and sent East.

I saw children snatched out of the hands of some of the parents.

Fresh food stopped in the western area and was diverted to the East. The fertile became barren and the barren became fertile.

All this, from Just One Roar of the Lion.

I saw 3 long lines of writing in the sky. It read:

Lost, Lost, Lost.

But below it I saw the word:
Gain , gain, gain…….. where this line ended I could not see, as it just continued on, endlessly.

I saw that the East gained money, food, etc.

The losses were loss of power, prestige, money, position.

I saw:

Where a soldier stood to load his gun, to shoot, even the last single bullet he had was taken away.

Where a soldier stood ready for packing his gun, where truce had been declared, divine bullets loaded his gun, and led him to shoot.

In the Universe, expected cosmic events were diverted and unexpected ones were brought forth.

Deserts bloomed, greenery was made barren. Light that had focused on the West, now moved East.

This was so sudden that it was like saying… "One morning I woke up, and all was changed".

(Scripture: Amos 3:8):
"The lion hath roared, who will not fear? The Lord God hath spoken, who can but prophecy?"

The Lion has Roared.

Dark clouds disintegrated from one place and gathered in another.

Whilst there was a West to East exchange on a large level, on individual levels there were changes too. Everything, everything, everything, was changing.

All this from Just One Roar of the Lion.

Just that One Roar, and things from here, were flying there and vice versa. People/ Nations, who had got used to a way of life/ of thinking, were in for either a shock or a surprise.

CHANGE, CHANGE, CHANGE, CHANGE, CHANGE, CHANGE, CHANGE.

The hungry were fed, and the fed, went hungry. All opposites were happening. Many homeless were housed, and many of those with homes, became homeless. Light became dark and dark became light. Whatever the present situation, the opposite was happening.

Many rich became poor and many of the poor became rich.

All this, from Just One Roar of the Lion.

Clouds that were meaning to rain, suddenly disintegrated and it rained elsewhere, where least expected.

People were in puzzlement. They said to themselves, "But I thought…." No nothing would be as "I thought."

Many were saying, "But it always worked this way". Now no more. For those who said, "It's never worked for me," they were surprised to know that it will, now.

Heralds blew trumpets, proclaiming: "End of empire, end of empire".

Anyone who had been a Specialist, Monopolist, the kingpin in any area of his life/business, now that would begin to end. Nations that had empires or aspirations building towards it, would now see the beginning of the end of those empires.

Nothing was the same. Everything, everything had changed.

Just One Roar Of The Lion.

And He Has Roared.

Empty pockets were filled, the filled emptied.

Strategic changes were taking place. Whatever had worked like clockwork, would not work now. People of peace were making war, and warring nations calmed down.

For the warring nations it was like the wind was taken out of their sails.

Just as Egypt, Persia, Babylon, Rome, Britain, etc, were all once super powers/empires, but their reign and era ended, so now any 'super power'/ or aspirations thereof, was being diffused. Nations that were looked up to were now beginning to be looked down upon and vice versa.

Balance of power and favor had shifted East.

Angels in the West, held Gold Books. One book was titled "Most Wanted", the other, "Most Favored".

'The Most Wanted' Book had living photographs of the most evil people, the traitors etc. Each one was dealt with and disposed.

The Most Favored, in the other gold Book with living photographs, were some of those, who had lived through most desolate conditions, such were lifted up.

(All that is related here, remember was happening all at once.)

In the midst of all this, I heard the Angels sing: Glory, Glory, Glory.

Time was speeded up in some places, in others, it was slowed down. Wild beasts were all crouching in fear, afraid. I saw the milk inside of cows, curdle.

Just One Roar Of the Lion.

I saw Angels collect gold crowns from those in the North, and they dipped the crowns in a smoky place (the kind of smoke one sees with dry ice), when the crowns emerged from the smoke, they looked exactly the same, but now they were silver.

No matter in which direction I looked all had changed.

It seemed that the very nature of nature changed.

Volcanoes that were dormant, the ashes were removed, and a new fire was lit in them. It seemed that certain species suddenly became extinct.

Reams of paper fell from the sky; paper and pens were sent down, for Chroniclers and Historians, for it was going to be a busy time for them.

Nothing of all creation was left untouched, at Just One Roar of The Lion.

Outside, the earth looked still, but within were rapid-fire changes.

Quick, sudden, some were devastating, others surprisingly favorable, but this favor was mostly for the East.

I saw what looked like a flight-path that normally airlines describe on their brochures, as routes of flights/destinations.

For prophets, their flight-paths were moved from here to there, as if randomly, but it was not random, it was the Plan of God for prophets. Prophets will be suddenly moved, and see things from a new vantage point.

I saw some people become tar, whilst others became fountains of water.

Just One Roar Of The Lion.

Many changes took place in the Universe.

On earth, snows of old melted, and water in unlikely places froze.

It is no ordinary thing, when the Lion Roars.

Those dressed warm in the winter, had their clothes taken away, they were left naked. But the naked street-dweller was clothed. There was a divine transfer of wealth, knowledge, and understanding.

People, who'd talked and talked for years, had their mouths taped. But as in Ezekiel 24: 27, those that had been mute for a season, now spoke.

As the vision progressed, I heard the Lord Say: "My People have no roof over their head. I Am their Roof."

I was flown speedily, over building after building, and as we flew, I heard the Lord Say: "Not Mine, not Mine, not Mine, not Mine, not Mine, not Mine, not Mine."

Now I was despairing. What then was God's?

Then I was shown, people in the fields, with instruments. They had no roof over their heads. These were God's own.

The buildings we flew over, were demolished by an elephant's trunk and many T.V. Studios had a fire underneath them. Apparently these buildings had been re-built on the same grounds where prior buildings had been condemned and burnt. These new buildings had been built on the foundations of charred remains, and ashes.

All that was up to the present became obsolete, and new technology, the secrets of which were hidden in nature, appeared.

Science made simple but profound discoveries. I saw Scientists have a 'Eureka' moment. For many who were researching, studying, looking for, the 'thing', it was right there before their very noses. Once they saw it they slapped their foreheads, lamenting, "Silly me!"

Follies of science were exposed. The simplicity of the discoveries to come, were mind-boggling.

Just One Roar Of The Lion.

The very nature of nature seemed to be changing. It was as unbelievable as Isaiah 11: 6-8, 'The wolf also shall dwell with the lamb, and the leopard shall lie down with the kid…"

In some places, I saw an overabundance of wheat, which flowed into the sea, as it was so plentiful. But in other places, I saw land, which was once green, and was now parched land, where nothing grew. I saw beautiful blooms on cactus/desert plants.

He, who understands these changes, will prepare.

The Earth was in a global eclipse. One half had light, the other half was in darkness. It seemed that plates were shifted/ removed from the earth. There were people who raged against God. "We'll do what we have to, let Him do what He wants to", they were saying.

Trees trembled. They knew that their time to be cut had come. To many, prophets and counselors were restored, but from others, the prophets and counselors departed. Sadly from those they departed, noticed it not.

Focus/ emphasis of the Church, and the world, due to the presence of new circumstances, changed.

All this, by Just One Roar Of The Lion.

[Source – tentsofissachar.wordpress.com. Used by permission]

CHAPTER FIVE

OUT OF THE WILDERNESS

The 'wilderness' is not a concept that is understood too well in Christendom today, despite the fact that it is all the way through the Bible. From the book of Genesis right through Revelation there are clear references to the wilderness as being something God often employs in His dealings with men. The pattern is undeniable.

But why does God use it so often? And why is a spiritual wilderness so necessary? What is its purpose and how does it change us?

When we look through the Scriptures we see that the wilderness is often a place of spiritual crisis and also preparation. It is the place God sends us before the "real action" begins – before we enter into the full purposes of God in our lives. There must be 'death' before there can be resurrection. There must be a desert place before the "promised land".

The wilderness is a place of trial and testing, of brokenness and full surrender to God. The props and activities that have kept us continually striving to "make things happen" are stripped away. Our self-reliance is shattered and replaced with a total reliance on God alone. Every "idol" in our lives (often including our own ministry) is brought under the piercing searchlight of God. Our selfish motives and ambitions are shown for what they are.

This process may take years. Finally we emerge broken, chastened and purified. The process has matured and cleansed us in so many ways. We are now ready for the fulfillment of all that God originally called us to do. But our heart-motives are vastly different from what they were before. Like many others, I myself have experienced a number of wilderness periods in my life – which were often very painful at the time. But I know now how essential they were in preparing me for the work I have ahead of me today.

INTO THE DESERT

As I said, we see this pattern all the way through Scripture. Many lessons can be learned from what we read there. Let's take a look at some examples:

The story of Joseph from the book of Genesis is one that has 'wilderness' written all over it. Joseph was the favored son in his family, and had been given dreams by God of his destiny as a true leader among his people. Yet little did he realize that the path to this destiny was one of betrayal, pain, rejection and imprisonment.

In fact, an essential factor in this story was the jealousy of Joseph's brothers, who sold him into slavery in Egypt. If they had not done this, then it is doubtful that his God-given dreams would ever have come to pass. Even after Joseph got to Egypt the nightmare continued. He was thrown into jail for years, for a crime he did not commit. All this time, God was breaking him and molding him to be the true leader that he was to become. For it is only in the desolate places that God is able to do this deep preparation work.

Then all of a sudden after years and years, in one day Joseph went from prison to palace! Because of his God-given wisdom in interpreting the dreams of Pharaoh, Joseph was made Prime Minister over all Egypt – second only to the king. His years of suffering in the wilderness were over. A new season had begun. A season in which he would see every promise that God had given him fulfilled.

ANOTHER EXAMPLE

Probably the best-known instance of a wilderness experience in the Old Testament is the story of Moses and the children of Israel. There are some important lessons in this one as well. We all know the story. Moses had been raised and trained all his life in the palaces of Egypt. But when he came face-to-face with his heritage as an Israelite, he rose up "in his own strength" and killed an Egyptian slave-driver. He was then forced to flee into the desert, where he was to spend 40 years as a simple shepherd.

What an enormous length of time! Imagine if every Christian leader had to spend that long in the wilderness before God would allow them to lead His people! It is almost impossible to imagine the depths of despair and "death" to all his dreams and hopes that Moses went through during this time. In fact, after 40 years it is hard to imagine anyone being "deader" to the usual ambitions and temptations of leadership than Moses would have been. And what PATIENCE these years of waiting must have produced in him!

Again we see here the lengths that God will go to in the "preparation" phase of a leader (though 40 years is unusually long). The isolation, the chafing, the crying out to God for deliverance – all play their part. Such an experience is almost irreplaceable. That is why God uses it so often. The hearts of driven men are so similar in so many ways, that God's "cure" becomes similar also. He will even shut us up in a kind-of 'prison' for a time so we cannot escape the process. It is that important. He does not want self-oriented leaders shepherding his precious sheep.

DEEP DEALINGS

After his 40 years of preparation, Moses returned to Egypt at God's command to lead His people out of bondage. This was the beginning of the entire nation of Israel's wilderness experience. For when they left Egypt the only way to their Promised Land was through the desert. Some commentators say that in a straight line, their journey could have taken just a few weeks or less. But because of their disobedience and fear, the vast majority of those who left Egypt were destined to die in the desert, never reaching the Promised Land. In fact, their wilderness journey ended up taking 40 years!

Now we need to take special note of this fact:- Not everyone who entered the wilderness survived it. In fact, multitudes perished there. The wilderness tried them and found them wanting. They went to the place of testing and failed the test. This is a pretty crucial fact to realize in our day also. Just because we are "called out" and enter a wilderness time, does not mean that we will embrace the dealings of God and respond appropriately. It is entirely possible to lose everything out there. These people lost out completely. Only their children came through to inherit the promises of God.

PROPHETS & THEIR MESSAGE

The Old Testament makes it clear that it was not just future leaders that God trained in the wilderness. Most of His prophets were prepared for their ministry in these places of desolation as well. Every would-be Elijah or Elisha of God must go through such times of intense spiritual training. And this is true not just of the Old Testament but also of the New. In fact, to this day, if there is one type of ministry that is most associated with the concept of wilderness it is "Prophetic" ministry. And I believe that there is a strong prophetic aspect to a lot of what we have seen with "wilderness" experiences today.

We could give examples of desert experiences for many of the Old Testament prophets. But I think that one of the most interesting prophets to look at is John the Baptist, the man who prepared the way for the New Testament era. Jesus declared that, "Among them that are born of women there has not risen one greater than John the Baptist." And yet, after thirty years of preparation, the duration of his ministry was to be only six months! But what a six months it was.

The Bible tells us that John was hidden in the desert places until the time of his showing-forth came. Suddenly he arrived, as if from nowhere, with a piercing word of repentance on his lips. His sermons were among the most fiery of any prophet in history. "And there went out unto him all the land of Judea, and they of Jerusalem, and were all baptized of him in the river of Jordan, confessing their sins" (Mk 1:5).

It is important to remember that Jesus too went through a wilderness period just before His ministry began. As we all know, when he was baptized the Holy Spirit descended upon Him like a dove. "Then was Jesus led by the Spirit into the wilderness to be tempted by the devil" (Mt 4:1). This wilderness period was a time of testing and trial, of fasting for 40 days and nights, and of relentless attacks from the enemy. When Jesus had made it through to the other end, He was truly ready to begin His ministry. Thus, even in the life of the Savior of the world, the wilderness was a crucial milestone.

It is astonishing just how many of God's future leaders and spokesmen were sent into this place of aloneness and brokenness before being brought into their true destiny. We have not even mentioned heroes of God such as Noah, Joshua, Jacob, Job and others who all had similar experiences. Part of this process lies in the "waiting" that takes place. Also, the fact that all the supporting props are taken away. The waiting alone can be torture.

The wilderness also deals with any fear of man or 'systemized' way of looking at things. God often uses it to bring a whole fresh perspective, which is very important for leaders who are going to be representing a "new" approach or facing opposition because of the confrontational words that they are bringing. The lonely desert years give them backbone to stand up to the crowd or the powers-that-be, and declare God's truth without compromise. They now truly fear God rather than man. And they think differently from others. The wilderness is vital for anyone who is wanting to bring fresh manna to God's people.

MODERN EXPERIENCES

Below are a number of interesting emails I received relating to this topic:

From: Scott (-USA):

We're quick to equate "The Wilderness" to a negative thing. I don't believe that. I believe that some of what God is getting ready to do, some of it can't be taught from the pulpit. The old expression, "It can't be taught, it has to be caught" plays a large part of this.

"And the child grew, and waxed strong in spirit, and WAS IN THE DESERTS till the day of his showing unto Israel" (Lk 1:80). There was an order change getting ready to happen... John the son of Zacharias was not going to learn that truth in his father's home, nor in church on the Sabbath. It was a revelation that came while John was in the wilderness. What God was getting ready to do, the move of God that was getting ready to unfold (Jesus) had to be taught somewhere outside of the influence and the order of that day.

I believe there is an order change coming to the church today, just like in the days of John. I don't mean some new order of salvation or grace. I mean in the church. We've produced a lot of stuff that Jesus didn't have anything to do with. I believe the change of order will bring God's order back to His people. And I believe that God has those that He calls sons in those "wilderness" places because He's getting ready to impart and deposit something into their hearts that quite possibly can't be taught in the church today...

I'm not saying that the church is all screwed up. I love the church. I attend every week. I believe those in the wilderness love the church as well. I believe they are there at the prompting of the Holy Spirit. There are things and truths that God is opening them up to that can't be taught within the 4 walls of the church right now.

In your article, you mentioned that "thousands are already opting out. And many feel like they are 'waiting' for something." I believe that! I believe they're there with expectation. Fasting, praying, listening for the voice of God. I doubt many of them even understand why. But just by gut level faith, they believe Jesus has said, "Come away."

You mentioned that it's not possible for them to stay away forever. Agreed. I believe they will return and infiltrate the church. And bring with them a message and a revelation that will stagger us.

Obviously, there are those who will use "hurts, wounds" as reasons to walk away and not be responsible. Others are just plain lazy and carnal. But there are those who have heard the voice of the Master compelling them to seek his face and his heart outside the 4 walls of the local church.

From: Hari (-Australia):

The wilderness is a place void of distractions and pomp and fanfare, a place where the Lord alone awaits you. It has been 5 years to date and during that time we have attempted to 'get back in' but somehow we keep getting shoved 'right back out'.... We are not embittered, we are not unsubmitted but we are disillusioned.

You have to sometimes be on the outside to actually see what is going on. To be of help to a man trapped in the pit you have to be outside in order to pull him out. Of course being 'outside' is in itself an open sore to those 'inside'. It brings to the surface many questions that simply will not lay down, that do not want to be faced.

But in this wilderness we have found Him and He alone has led and fed us and caused us to grow in such a way that a thousand lifetimes of church meetings could never achieve. Perhaps like John the Baptist we are all awaiting a call to come out and go into the cities (Lk 3:2) and like him we will be a people prepared to prepare the way for His coming... Perhaps then the world will see something different, perhaps then we will once again be a people that 'turn the world upside down'.

From: Donna (-USA):

Lately I have come to understand that it is in the desert that the highway is prepared... I do not know exactly what my Father has planned for me, but it is something far beyond anything I can imagine. I do know that there is a revelation of restored truth that is coming to many in the desert that soon will be released. All should be making the purchases of Revelation 3:18, particularly the eye salve. Not all things come by grace – there is a price to be paid by those who would overcome.

From: Shearon (-USA):

Politics doesn't belong in the church, choirs on parade don't belong in the church, hat day doesn't belong in the church, etc. We have gotten away from what the church is all about. Lord take us back.

I too have gone through a wilderness experience so I can relate to what they are going through. The wilderness isn't easy, we should all have one. The wilderness has a purpose, I thank God for my experience, I learned so much. But yes, you are right, there is a time to come out. You can't stay in the wilderness (yes, I wanted to). There is a time when God will send you out, like He did with Moses and His Son. It may be 40 days, it may be 6 months, or it may be 40 years, but you must come out. If not, what was it for?

From: Bryan Hupperts (-USA):

"And you shall remember all the way which the Lord your God has led you in the wilderness (desert) these forty years, that he might humble you, testing you, to know what was in your heart, whether you would keep his commandments or not." - Deut. 8: 2

Look at the history of God's dealings with his saints... Paul spent years in the desert before his commissioning as an Apostle. God has used the drought of many deserts to forge some of His finest saints.

Deserts are such obscure places. They precede blessing but are themselves looked upon as curses. They function to bring you to the place of having to only concern yourself with the basics of existence. It is when water, symbolic of the Living Word of God, becomes the only issue of your life, what you live and die by, are you finally ready to enter into the Master's service. One drop from heaven is all you need. When all else in this world appears as sand in your eyes, empty barren waste, you are ready for Kingdom service.

Deserts have the curious effect of hardening your resolve while humbling your heart before God... When you can blossom with just a little water, you can blossom anywhere! After the desert, you will be "like a tree planted by the water" thriving!..

Don't curse the desert times. God is testing you, seeing what is in your heart. Actually, he is letting you see what He has seen all along. Allow your roots to grow deep into God so that "out of your belly shall gush forth rivers of living water." A river in the desert suddenly springing forth? Sure, that's His way.

God often uses the desert to prepare the messenger. When the messenger is ready, then the message comes. We have our part to prepare ourselves for the ministries God calls us to. We also have to be prepared by God for those same tasks. When we can serve Him in a place of barrenness, we can serve Him in a place of fruitfulness. It is when we are humbled and broken of our own power that God can then show Himself strong on our behalf.

UP FROM THE WILDERNESS

As stated earlier in this book, I believe a new era in God is opening up and He is calling many who have been waiting in the wilderness to be part of it. Sometimes people get so used to the desert that they begin to grow comfortable in it – and thus they are not ready for the risks involved in taking the Promised Land. What is needed today are the Joshuas and Calebs who can not only survive the wilderness but who also have a "war-like" spirit – hungry for their moment to take new ground. And take it they will.

Years ago in August 2006, a woman named Hollie Moody who had received a large number of remarkable prophecies and visions was given the following word – which I believe may well apply to the very hour we are in:

IT IS TIME FOR THEE, LORD, TO WORK!
-extracts by Hollie L. Moody

The Lord asked me a question a while ago that at the time I thought was a bit strange. He asked me if I would have liked John the Baptist if I had met him in person? After thinking about this question for a while, I had to honestly admit I probably would not have cared too much for John the Baptist if I had met him in person. He was not a diplomatic person. He did not seem to be very gentle or loving. He was uncouth, rough in his manner of speech and dress. His appearance most likely was as off-putting as his manner of speech was.

Yet, the people of his day flocked to hear him preach. I had to ask myself, "Why?" What was it the people went out into the wilderness to see and hear?

There are a people whom the Lord has been preparing in the wilderness. They will shortly be appearing upon the religious and spiritual scene. And, for the most part, they will be as John the Baptist may have been: uncouth, undiplomatic, and rough in their manner of speech and dress. They will not be well liked.

Jesus Himself asked the people what they went into the wilderness to see when they went to hear John the Baptist. "A reed shaken with the wind? A man clothed in soft raiment?" No, Jesus testified of John. The people went into the wilderness to see and to hear a prophet. (Matthew 11:7-15.)

There has been much talk for years about spiritual wildernesses. After a season of glory, for many of God's children, they appeared to be driven into a wilderness setting spiritually. Jesus Himself was driven into the wilderness by the Spirit immediately after a voice from heaven testified of Who He was.

What transpired to Jesus while He was in the wilderness? Temptation. Testing. Aloneness. And, eventually, victory over His flesh and His will. After Jesus successfully withstood the temptations of the devil, and only then, angels came and ministered unto Him.

For those who have felt driven by the Spirit into a spiritual wilderness, they have learned while in the wilderness that the Lord is still with them. God has still been sustaining and feeding them spiritually. They have been given spiritual manna to feast upon.

However, I feel led to caution those who have been feasting upon spiritual manna in the wilderness that the time to come out of the wilderness has arrived. The Lord will no longer be providing spiritual manna in the wilderness. To continue to try and be sustained by this spiritual manna, to remain in the wilderness, will now only bring about rottenness and spiritual death.

Exodus 16:19-20 ~ "And Moses said, Let no man leave of it till the morning. Notwithstanding they hearkened not unto Moses; but some of them left of it until the morning, and it bred worms, and stank: and Moses was wroth with them."

There is the sound of voices crying out in the wilderness. Those who hear the sound of these voices, will live spiritually.

John 1:23 ~ "He said, I am the voice of one crying in the wilderness, Make straight the way of the Lord, as said the prophet Esaias."

There are two groups of people who will emerge from the wilderness.

The first group who will withdraw from their spiritual wildernesses will do so with little to none recognition of their having done so by those around them. These are the ones who have become prayer warriors in the wilderness. They have been completely stripped of all fleshly desires for the recognition and/or approval of man.

In the wilderness, they have learned the importance of the Body of Christ. All that they will do, will be for the greater health and maturity of the Church. They will not be known. They will not be recognized. They will not have the approval of others. They will suffer, and do so in silence as they pray forth a great outpouring of God's glory.

Matthew 6:6 ~ "But thou, when thou prayest, enter into thy closet, and when thou hast shut thy door, pray to thy Father which is in secret; and thy Father which seeth in secret shall reward thee openly."

The second group of people to emerge from the wilderness, will have the prayers of the first group as their foundation. This second group will be used to bring forth a miraculous and mighty move of God's Spirit. Unbelief will hinder some from being a part of this miraculous move of God's Spirit. The stone of unbelief must be removed in order for us to behold this miraculous move of God's Spirit.

Romans 15:19 ~ "Through mighty signs and wonders, by the power of the Spirit of God; so that from Jerusalem, and round about unto Illyricum, I have fully preached the gospel of Christ."

CHAPTER SIX

RISE OF THE DAVIDS

As you have doubtless picked up by now, no revivalist that I have ever studied was a "popularity"-oriented, or man-pleasing type of leader. (In fact, usually quite the opposite). These were certainly not men to be trifled with. They knew when to be gentle, but were also never afraid to "reprove, rebuke and exhort" with all Godly authority where necessary. They were strong yet balanced leaders – firm but fair. Their love for God and for the people (in that order) enabled them to make allowances for people's frailties, but also meant that they never gave the devil an inch.

Such anointed leaders as these are sorely needed in our day, and there can be no doubt that this is exactly the kind of leadership that is about to arise in the coming revival. (For God must have His "mighty men and women of valor" as always – His Joshuas, Elijahs, Deborahs, Davids, Pauls, Luthers, Wesleys, etc).

What I want to do in this chapter is to take a fresh look at the story of David, Saul and Jonathan, from a slightly new perspective. One of the main focuses, of course, will be the tremendous godly attributes that this man David had. Just like in the last chapter, David suffered through his own "wilderness" that ended up being essential to his eventual success. But it was a long and torturous process that took many years.

You will no doubt recall how King Saul had fallen into compromise, presumption and rebellion, and that the prophet Samuel had told Saul that the kingdom would be taken from him and given to another. The prophet then went and anointed David to be the future king. However, there was to be a time of waiting and preparation before David could assume the leadership of Israel. It is my belief that this equates directly to the current situation.

I believe that there is definitely a "David company" of future leaders whom God has been preparing in secret for many years around the world. Most of those who are part of this company will already know who they are. Many of them will have received their first or even their second anointing (remembering that David was anointed three times before he became leader of all Israel), and will probably already be operating in their calling to some degree.

LEADERS OF TOMORROW

One thing is certain: This will be a company of prophetic people – people whom God has been speaking to about the things to come. Such people will often have great difficulty fitting into the present system, for essentially they will have been designed for tomorrow's church, rather than today's. They will often feel like misfits, and may be misunderstood, persecuted and maltreated by those who identify themselves strongly with the present order. Often the powers-that-be will see them as some kind of threat.

Such was the case with David. For years Saul's jealousy and rage caused him to have to flee for his life. Pursued relentlessly by Saul and his men, David was forced to hide out in caves, in the desert, and for a time even among the Philistines! How hurt and lonely he must have felt at times. Here he was, the one whom Samuel had anointed to be the future king, now an outcast, persecuted, maltreated, slandered... And this went on for years.

Remember, Saul was still king over Israel, even though he had already been rejected by God. He was still positioned as the leader of God's people. Now here is the crucial question: What was David's attitude toward Saul all this time? The answer is very revealing: David was utterly constant in his genuine respect and honor toward him. He would make no move to try and wrest the leadership away from Saul (as he could have done). He was very aware of God's timing, and he would make no move to circumvent it.

Twice he could easily have killed Saul and the kingdom would have been his, but he chose instead to demonstrate real honor and love toward him. When news reached David that Saul was dead, he wept and mourned over him. He had still held out hope for Saul, and had treated him as the rightful leader of God's people, right up to the day that Saul died.

It is my belief that by-and-large, there are essentially three types of leaders or ministries operating in today's Christian world: the Sauls, the Jonathans and the Davids. Let us look at each of these in a little more detail (and I warn you, I will be very 'frank' in this):

1. THE SAULS. These are the Christian leaders who have firmly aligned themselves with the present order, with its compromise, its institutional control, it's rejection of seeking true holiness, it's love of "pleasures" more than love of God, etc. Sadly, such leaders will often welcome any new Christian fad, so long as it doesn't cost them too much, and so long as it helps keep people involved in the church. (This is why they have often welcomed new "church growth" methods, etc).

Beyond this, however, they stand firmly for the status quo. The thought of true reformation would absolutely horrify most of them (which is why they will oppose or persecute any genuine 'Davids' that they can identify). And when the new David-type ministries arise in their church, they will often attempt to "stomp" on them, to dominate them, or if that doesn't work, to limit their influence as much as possible.

To the Sauls of today I believe God would have me say: Because you have made yourselves "lords" over the church in Jesus' stead, God will snatch the royal scepter from your hands. And because of the compromise that has been found in your mouths for so long, God will lay much of the blame for the sickly state of today's "lukewarm" church directly at your feet. You have been rejected by God as being unfit to lead His people. "The kingdom shall be taken from you and given unto another" (See Mt 21:43, 1 Sa 15:22-23, 1 Sa 28:17, etc). "Behold, you despisers, and wonder, and perish: for I work a work in your days, a work which you shall in no way believe, though a man declare it unto you" (Acts 13:41).

It is interesting to note that the most serious sin that Saul committed in God's eyes (the sin that finally caused him to be rejected by God as unfit to lead His people) was that after the battle with the idolatrous Amelikites, Saul compromised what God had said by allowing his men to take the best of the enemy flocks as spoil, instead of killing them all.

This 'men-pleasing', rebellious disregard for God's word, caused Saul to be immediately told that his kingdom would be taken from him. "For rebellion is as the sin of witchcraft, and stubbornness is as iniquity and idolatry. Because you have rejected the word of the Lord, He has also rejected you from being king" (1 Sa 15:23). Notice that it was not Saul's 'control' or domination of the people that caused him to be rejected by God, but rather his weakness and compromise as a leader (ie. his desire to be pleasing and accommodating toward his people at the expense of God's word). Is it not the same today also?

2. THE JONATHANS. You will no doubt remember that Jonathan, who was Saul's son, had a tremendous devotion and love for David. They were like brothers. While Saul went about trying to kill David, Jonathan was doing his best to quietly protect and help him. I believe there are quite a number of leaders and ministries around the world today who are just like Jonathan. They have definitely been "friends" of the true revival, But like Jonathan they are caught between their allegiance to the 'old' or existing order, and their affinity with the new ministries – the "Davids".

They want to be part of the great Reformation that God is about to send, but they are just too attached to the old system and the old ways to really let go. (Compromise again!) This is a very dangerous position to be in – in a very real way, just as dangerous as that of Saul. For it is very significant that even though Jonathan was a friend of David (ie. a friend of the new move of God), he was killed on the same battlefield and on the same day that Saul was killed. Jonathan never got to see or enter into the new move of God at all (ie. the reign of David). In essence, he suffered exactly the same fate as Saul.

Another thing that is significant about Jonathan was that he was the "heir apparent" (ie. the 'obvious' choice to lead Israel in the new era, when Saul was gone). I believe that many of today's Jonathans are also like this. They are the seemingly 'obvious' revival-oriented leaders of today – the kind of men who preach on revival, prophecy and prayer, etc, but in an "acceptable" kind of way. Many of them are truly prophetic, but they fit into the current set-up just a little too well. They have a reputation to uphold in the existing system, and they can be trusted not to say anything too radical, or to rock today's "Laodicean" boat too hard. They are certainly nothing like the stench in Saul's nostrils that David was. No-one feels particularly 'threatened' by their presence.

As I have said, I believe that there are quite a number of Jonathans in ministry all over the world today. The greatest danger for them is that because of their current respectability and their attachment to the existing order, they just can't imagine God bringing judgment upon the very systems and 'streams' that they have formed relationships with. They love David and all that he stands for, but they just cannot let go of Saul. Deep in their heart they are still clinging to a kind of "acceptable" amalgam between both the existing order and also the new move of God. (It will never happen).

Today's Jonathans would be quite happy if the 'new wine' could somehow be crammed into the old wineskins. They have their feet in both camps. And the terrible likelihood is that when the day of decision dawns, when that fateful hour arrives, because of their double-mindedness they will surely be found with Saul, rather than David. And this can only result in tragedy. Their failure to see the signs that it is time to finally abandon Saul, and throw in their lot entirely with David, means that they will surely be caught up in the very judgment that falls upon Saul. Sadly, all the signs are there that the cry, "How have the mighty fallen" is about to ring out again in our day.

3. THE DAVIDS. As we have seen, by and large, the reign of king Saul was not a particularly happy time for David. However, I believe that this long, enforced period of brokenness and humility in David's life was absolutely essential in preparing him to become a truly godly leader of Israel. It was at this time that David could easily have become a 'rebel', deliberately stirring up dissension against Saul in retaliation for the way he was being treated.

Remember, David had already been anointed by Samuel as the future leader of Israel. He was a renowned warrior, a natural leader, a mighty man of valor. If he had wanted to, he and his men could have stirred up a great deal of trouble for Saul. But instead, with great patience and forbearance, David endured all things, respecting Saul's authority, not murmuring or causing dissension against him, etc. And I truly believe that as much as possible we are to be like David in our attitude towards the church leaders in our own situations today.

Even though there must have been times when David felt extremely distressed, angry and hurt at Saul's treatment of him, he never allowed this to become a festering wound of resentment that would cause him to react in rebellion against Saul. I truly believe that if David had acted out of rebellion, then he may well have proved himself unworthy of his calling to lead God's people. I do not believe that God ever sanctions rebellion. In fact, as we have seen, it was because of rebellion that Saul had been rejected as king in the first place. I believe that God was watching David to make sure that this kind of rebellion was not found in him also. And of course, He is watching us for the exact same reason.

I am convinced that God would have even the 'Sauls' among today's Christian leaders treated with genuine respect and honor, right up until God Himself acts to strip their authority, and to anoint and raise up the Davids in their place. (Please note: It is GOD who will do this, in His own perfect time). Until then, I believe we are to willingly give today's leaders genuine honor and loyalty as befitting God's appointed leaders over His people.

We are also to genuinely love them and pray for them. Remember, David mourned and wept over Saul when he died. What depths of godliness this man David had! And I firmly believe that God is calling the Davids of today to be of this same spirit. We are certainly not to be like Absolem, who sat in the gates of the city some years later, murmuring and subtly turning the people to rebellion against king David. Rebellion is sin, and every one of us needs to ask God to search our hearts to see if there be any "wicked way", any dark seed of rebellion, found in us.

In saying all of this, I do not want people to think that I am advocating some kind of abject, unthinking "slave-submission" to leaders (where you don't "think" – you just do what you are told). This is certainly not the kind of relationship that David had with Saul. In fact, while David was utterly constant in his genuine honor and respect for Saul, he also did his best to avoid him as much as possible, even when Saul assured him that he would be safe!

David and Saul were of opposing spirits, and "how can two walk together unless they be agreed?" They were by no means real friends or natural allies. This is the way it has always been between these two opposite types of leaders. One walks under God's special favor, and the other (who once knew this divine favor himself) now does not, and in their heart of hearts they both know it. (Which is why the 'Sauls' are so jealous).

It is also important to note that after Saul had 'died' (ie. had his authority and anointing finally stripped by God), David was appointed as king of Judah (ie. as the anointed and recognized leader of his own tribe). After being anointed to lead Judah, David now had no hesitation in waging war on the descendants of Saul for the leadership of the entire nation of Israel.

This was no longer rebellion. David was now the only rightful, God-appointed leader of the whole kingdom, and it was time for him to "take it by force". As the Scriptures tell us, "There was a long war between the house of Saul and the house of David; and David grew stronger and stronger, while the house of Saul became weaker and weaker" (2 Sam 3:1).

THREE ANOINTINGS

It is interesting to note the order of events that led from David as shepherd-boy to David as God-appointed leader of a united and powerful Israel. In those early preparation days as a shepherd (an ideal role), David learned to faithfully care for those he had been given charge over, and to defend them fearlessly from the ravaging 'bears and lions', etc. As Jesus said centuries later, "You have been faithful over a little, I will set you over much" (Mt 25:21).

It was now that David received his first 'kingly' anointing, by the hand of the prophet Samuel. He then burst onto the public scene in quite spectacular fashion (the victory over Goliath), but quickly found himself offside with the existing leadership, and was forced into hiding. After many years as an outcast, with Saul finally 'dead', David received his second kingly anointing, and became king of Judah, from whence he waged war on the descendants of Saul for leadership of the whole nation of Israel.

David was finally anointed as leader of all Israel some years later. Under his leadership, Israel became a united, powerful, victorious nation, mighty in battle and utterly glorifying to God – displaying

His grace and glory to all nations. This is exactly what the coming move of God will bring about also. All of this is the exact purpose and reason for the coming reformation and revival. Glory to God! Jesus is returning for a Bride that is "without spot or wrinkle or any such thing."

One of the things that I most want people to take note of in the story of David and Saul is the vital importance of waiting for God's perfect time and for His anointing before we move. We see this principle so clearly in the life of David. This is why I want to encourage all of you who are reading this to wait until God moves before you try "pulling down the old", etc. We must await His perfect time.

I BELIEVE IN LEADERS!

Something I want to establish very strongly here is that the coming new leaders must never be afraid to truly "lead" God's people. If God appoints you to lead, then lead!

Over the last 30 years or so, I have often moved in circles in which it has been emphasized that any future revival must have "no superstars and no personalities". Sounds good! Obviously, all the glory must go to God, and self-promotion, pride and the idolizing of human leadership must have no place. But very often, I have found that this whole "no superstars, no personalities" thing has been taken much further, into the realm of basically desiring that there be no real leaders at all.

So what do we actually mean by this? Do we mean to say that God is now finished with "men of valor" – the Joshuas, the Gideons, the Peters or Pauls of ages past? Are we really now to have a kind of "leaderless" revival, as some have stated? (Declaring that God has little need for real leaders at all, and that He Himself will do all the leading, with almost no requirement for earthly shepherds). Sounds so right, doesn't it? So "spiritual" – so democratic. No superstars and no personalities. You have to admit, it has a nice ring to it.

The only problem is, if you take this concept to it's logical conclusion, then you have to do away with almost every major form of ministry found in the Bible – both Old and New Testaments. If God had operated this way in the past, then there would never have been a Moses or a Joshua, a Gideon or a Deborah, a David or a John-the-Baptist, a Peter or a Paul, a Martin Luther or a John Wesley, a William Booth or a Charles Finney (etc, etc). No heroes, no leaders, no apostles, no 5-fold ministry, no "mighty men" to lead God's people into war.

Let me ask you this question: Can we even have New Testament Christianity without the "5-fold" leadership of Ephesians 4 – building up the church? Is it even possible? Would there have been any book of Acts without the apostles? Didn't the early church "devote" itself to the apostles' teaching? If there are no shepherds, teachers, evangelists, prophets or apostles, how can the body possibly be built up into the "full stature" described in Eph 4:11-13?

For me personally, this whole question has been one that I have pondered at length over the years. And I have to admit that what God has shown me has caused me to adopt the exact opposite position to that which I formerly held. I can no longer believe in a "leaderless" revival. Everything that I have ever read about past moves of God, from the beginning of the Old Testament right down through recent revival history, has convinced me that this whole "leaderless" concept is a dangerous fallacy.

Not only is it almost entirely lacking in reason or historical legitimacy, but it actually goes against the very character of God and His dealings with men right down the ages. For God has always used men and women as His instruments to bring repentance, deliverance or revival to His people, and as carriers of His anointing – displaying His glory to a dying world. And He has always raised up strong leaders to establish and carry forward basically every new move that He has visited upon the earth. I am convinced that He is about to do so again, in the coming reformation.

THE WELSH REVIVAL

A true revival leader must never be 'soft' or compromising, but neither must he be harsh or authoritarian. He must be both a strong and a loving man of God – wise, patient, apt to teach, but also not afraid to "reprove, rebuke and exhort" where necessary. Above all else, in these mild and insipid times, he must not be afraid to be a true leader, despite what people say. History clearly demonstrates that with an absence of strong leadership, the devil gets in so fast that the coming move of God would probably only last a matter of months (if that).

What happened to the 1904 Welsh Revival after Evan Roberts (who was without a doubt one of God's great revivalists) suddenly disappeared from the scene, should be an object lesson to us all. Within a very short space of time after he was gone, the whole revival was being absolutely taken apart by the enemy, with no-one else around with the respect or authority to correct the excesses, expose the counterfeits, and keep the whole thing on the rails.

It seems that Evan Roberts (whose revival preaching was being reported by secular newspapers around the world) had been persuaded by certain parties that his prominence in the revival was somehow "stealing glory away from God". So, as a truly humble man, he took what he obviously thought was the most self-effacing or "spiritual" option available – he hid himself away in a small house, and refused to see anyone or to preach again for many years.

Thus, with God's true leader gone (the one with the true mantle and anointing, raised up by God to lead the revival), the devil now had free reign to 'spoil his goods'. In many ways this disaster could be likened to the children of Israel suddenly losing Moses after crossing the Red Sea, or losing Joshua just as they entered the promised land. The result was entirely predictable. Chaos! The devil had an absolute field-day, and the famous Welsh Revival, which should have been one of God's enduring victories, ended in relative disaster after little more than a year. Excesses and counterfeits flooded in, and thousands of young converts fell away (though many thousands still remained, and some new Pentecostal groups were able to emerge – so not all was lost).

I hope I am not being ungracious to the memory of one of God's great revivalists here. But I believe it is very important that we learn the lessons from this, and other moves of God down through history. The simple fact of the matter is: No leaders – no revival. If those whom God is calling to be leaders of a new move of God fail to truly "lead" it, then the devil is able to very easily undermine or destroy what God is doing. It is not "humble" to refuse to take authority and be a strong leader when God is calling you to do so. It is simply irresponsible and disobedient. And the same will be true of the coming move of God also.

The coming reformation/ revival will need strong leaders right from the start. And no doubt God has a hidden supply of these (as always), ready to take the field at His command. I also believe that in the coming move, new converts will grow up and fulfill their potential in God very rapidly. New ministries will arise and mature at a startling rate. He will raise up both the very young and the very old. After all, isn't this maturing of new, vigorous, anointed ministries one of the very reasons why God appoints leaders in His church (to bring them to maturity)? True leadership of God's flock has clearly always been a great privilege, but also an awesome responsibility.

WALKING IN POWER

Personally I can no longer believe in a Christianity without miracles – just like I cannot believe in a book-of-Acts church without miracles. Such a thing would be no Christianity at all. The early church had the power of God and so must we. Take this away and we no longer represent Christ fully – or His gospel.

The church I believe in is an invading force, a rampaging army, that cuts a swathe over the whole earth, "destroying the works of the devil". It is a people of great faith and ruthless determination, who batter down every 'gate' of hell and utterly destroy every stronghold, so the oppressed might be liberated and the captives be set free. This will be a Joshua army, commissioned by God to "take the land", to raze every work of Satan to the ground and utterly despoil the enemy camp. Like Jesus, they will "set their faces as flint" toward the Holy City, and nothing will stand in their path.

In saying all of this, however, I want to make it clear that I am not speaking of "taking over" the earth's political and educational systems, etc. This teaching (which is known as Dominion Theology) is quite widespread in some circles. However, the war that I am talking about is entirely "spiritual" – a war for the hearts and minds of men. As Jesus clearly stated, "My kingdom is not of this world" (John 18:36).

REFINING OF THE DAVIDS

In closing this chapter, I would just like to return briefly to our analogy of the Sauls, the Jonathans and the Davids. There can be no doubt that God has been preparing a "David company" of leaders to arise and lead His people in the coming move – leaders after His own heart who have been in hidden preparation for years.

However, a large number of these David-type ministries will probably have been badly stung by some of their dealings with the present Saulish system. As I have said, the Davids will almost always feel like misfits in the current church set-up. They are essentially designed to fit into the revived church of tomorrow rather than the Laodicean church of today.

Some of them will have received such a hammering whenever they have dared to speak up in the past, that they have now become quite 'crushed' and hesitant about sharing their convictions. Others will be feeling rather lonely – wondering if they are the only ones in their church who feel the way they do. There will be others again who, like David, have felt compelled to withdraw from the current system altogether, to a place of refuge far away from the Sauls. Still others may have felt called into the 'wilderness', just so that they can spend time alone with God, learning from Him. Believe me, I can sympathize with all of these.

However, I also believe that it is extremely vital that the Davids deal with any hurts, resentments, bitterness, rejection, or rebellion that have found a place in their hearts due to their unhappy dealings with churches or other authorities. Not only is this vitally important, but it is also urgent, I believe, because God is going to want to use these 'David' ministries in a great way very soon. For if the refining process is not complete, how can they hope to be a part of what God is about to do?

Every one of us needs to search our hearts to make sure that there is no deep root of resentment or rebellion lurking within us, as a result of our past dealings with authority figures (pastors, parents, etc), or other Christians.

These kinds of bad experiences can cause us to become "reactionary" – still reacting against these wounds many years later. Here are some sure signs of such reactionary strongholds in a person's life: They secretly enjoy hearing or seeing authority figures or institutions mocked or made a fool of. They can't seem to help 'murmuring' or complaining to others against particular authority figures that they know. (Motives are the things that need to be looked at here). This list could go on and on, but I am sure you get the idea. The "anti-authority" tendencies that some people have can be an awful limiting factor in their life.

How do we deal with such roots of rebellion deep within us? In exactly the same way as we deal with roots or strongholds of any other kind: We ask God to shed light on them, and then utterly 'RENOUNCE' them in the name of Jesus Christ, not just with our words, but also from the depths of our very being. We repent of them (with genuine godly sorrow) and COMMAND them gone in Jesus' name. One thing that true godly sorrow and deep repentance will always produce is a genuine hatred of sin, and this will bring abundant 'good fruit' into our lives.

BALANCE & MATURITY

As I said before, honoring and respecting authority does not necessarily mean abject, unthinking "submission" towards all leaders. We are not to be mindless 'slaves' to authority, but neither are we to ever be found among the rebellious "murmurers and complainers". God will help us judge what is right, if our hearts are pure before him. We are certainly not obliged to be loyal to any man who is leading us into blatant error. Really, I guess the best policy always is "balance in all things".

And just a short word here about the (often young) harsh, immature "prophet"-types who go around "blasting" people with bludgeoning, judgmental prophecies, etc. (I used to be one of these myself, as a very young man). Often, such 'prophets' may have a true calling on their life, but their immaturity, their (unknowing) pride and arrogance, and their secret rebellion make them very dangerous to themselves and to others. Until they allow God to bring true brokenness and humility into their lives (an often painful process), then they will usually end up causing more harm than good wherever they go.

There is a time for "rebuking" (though only experienced Christians should ever really consider it), but most of the time, there is no substitute for "speaking the truth in love". Wisdom, patience, gentleness, meekness and love should all be part of the 'strength' that God has built into our ministries. Otherwise we can end up doing great damage to His precious sheep. (For words can inflict great harm). Please think and pray about these things, my friends.

CHAPTER SEVEN

REFORMATION IN THE MEDIA

One of the worst problems the church has had in modern times is that the biggest 'Money' preachers on the planet have been able to buy their way onto television around the globe. This has had truly disastrous consequences – especially in places like Africa and South America. Since 2007 I have visited Nigeria and other African nations – and I can tell you, the damage that has been done by these Prosperity doctrines is truly enormous.

Many African preachers who start out genuinely serving the Lord are quickly corrupted by these Money teachings, and end up becoming total charlatans, manipulating their (often very poor) congregations and squeezing as much money out of them as they can. It is not uncommon to see these preachers riding around in Mercedes and BMW cars while their followers can barely afford the flip-flops on their feet.

All of this started in the 1980s when preachers like Kenneth Copeland, Benny Hinn and Creflo Dollar began to dominate Christian TV – which was soon being beamed by satellite into every poor country on earth. The Prosperity doctrine is a great way for preachers to raise large sums of money and Christian television operates on a "pay as you go" basis. Thus it allowed the greediest, most money-loving ministries to dominate – the ones who can raise the most cash by manipulating their audiences. These are the very ones who then buy all the TV time. And thus, much of the church worldwide has become deeply corrupted by Mammon.

It is difficult even to describe the enormity of this disaster to those who have not been to the Third World and seen the ugliness for themselves. The stomach-churning scope of this tragedy is almost beyond description. To me, it is one of the greatest challenges facing the end-time church.

No doubt you will remember the vision 'Just One Roar of the Lion' that was reprinted earlier in this book. In 2007 the author of that piece, Bombay lawyer Swarna Jha, also had another vision that relates to this very subject. Large extracts of it are below:

VISION: RAIDERS OF THE AIRWAYS
-extracts by Swarna Jha

I saw this vision around the end of November 2007...

High over America was a vast dome that covered the entire nation.

It looked like a giant spider's web.

As I looked closely I saw that most gaps had been filled with concrete and the web was now black with dust and dirt.

I saw that there were gaps, through which fresh air came in. The constant Broadcasting of filth had created the web, but I saw that there were those that did not broadcast filth, and the truth of their broadcasts was preventing the concrete spider's web from closing up completely.

There was Christian filth and non-Christian filth, being broadcast over the airways.

Those broadcasting the truth, when few wanted to hear it in the nation, were scattered and scant. Their voices were drowned out in the sounds of revelry and filth.

Those who loved the Lord, cried out to Him. Resources were scarce, and it was getting lonelier and lonelier being the 'lone' voice of truth in America. Oft times people had tried to gag them, other times, the Lord Had had them sit in silence.

Suddenly there was a deafening sound. The dome was caving in.

Raiders of the Airways, from other nations, were air-dropped into America, as were many armors, so that those God lovers, who had been or were yet to join broadcasting/publish/ or do anything media related, were protected in an armor that was fully kitted to do the Works of God.

As I looked at America, I saw that great changes were taking place in the media. I saw clenched fingers, held tightly in a fist, this was the fist of those who for years had controlled Christian/ non-christian media. I saw a wooden foot ruler (12 inch scale), descend from the sky and rap this clenched fist so hard, that the fingers were now no more tightly clenched, but they opened up. I understood within the vision, that monopolies in Media would be broken. As the fingers unfurled, I understood, that there would be openings, for new entrants, or the established smaller ones who were earlier considered 'inconsequential/ irrelevant,' into every form of media in areas where there had previously been an airtight control.

Underneath the surface, whilst media looked the same from above, below many changes were taking place. The tastes of many were changing. Quietly, from within, people were becoming more and more suspicious of media, it's style of reporting and the insult to the intelligence of the viewer/ hearer/ reader, by the programming. Christians and non-Christians were beginning to want something more substantial. Christians were becoming hungry for the Truth.

Those who had been making public their message of truth, in America were the Nathaniels, in whom was no guile. They spoke forthrightly, and many Americans accused them of being 'traitors', 'blasphemers' of the system the nation so revered.

These remnant in America who spoke the truth, at times felt lonely, rejected and many many times 'threw in the towel', for I saw a vision flash of the towel being thrown back at the remnant, by the Lord. God by His Grace had not allowed the remnant to give up, or resign. He Had Kept them going.

But now I saw in this vision that though on the surface American media looked exactly the same as it had done for years, underneath the surface many changes had already taken place and would continue.

God lovers had left the 'church' system and were compelled in their spirit to speak out against the lies, the false doctrines, the greedy leaders, the mammonites. They boldly aired their views and refuted the lies of the church and the government of the nation.

These Raiders of the airways, who constantly preached the truth and fought against the lies aired on TV, Radio, the Internet, the so-called 'churches', had by their ministry of countering such ever-increasing lies, slowly but surely found that they were not alone in the desire for hearing the truth. When these Raiders of the Airways had first begun to fight the lies, they did not do a 'market research' to see if there was a 'market' for the truth; they spoke, wrote, aired, and shared the truth, because they knew that they knew that truth MUST BE SHARED.

Whilst the dry-ones continued on writing and airing their E-manuals, knowing not EMMANUEL, these Raiders of the Airways, the truth lovers, spoke, wrote, shared, with some urgency all that the Lord had laid on their hearts. Their messages had been to prepare, to equip the saints for the coming hour.

Many in the land, due to the growing hunger for the truth in people, had grudgingly 'aired/shared' part truth on their forums, radio stations, Internet blogs, sites, forums, fearing like Saul, that if they did not do so the people would leave.

These compromisers had in this way, propagated mixture. From their platforms they shared false prophecies, and true prophecies, false doctrines and some true doctrines, so when their listeners and patrons heard/saw/read their 'wares' they became even more confused than before. Such 'vendors' of mixture did not understand that it would have been far better to shut down their sites, forums, radio/TV. stations than air such mixture. I saw that those hungry for the truth, slowly but surely moved away from those who persistently aired 'mixture.'

I saw that in America and world over, a process of elimination continued. People who sought the truth separated from the profane, they who were tickled, stuck with the filth.

The patrons/listeners/readers/viewers who remained with such as these became contributors of so much filth, that now the moderators/webmasters and TV and radio station owners, were despairing. They were trapped in the filth; the monsters they had created were now out of control.

Yet, donations from the undiscerning kept them going, and as they knew no other occupation but to vend filth and mixture, they would drag it as far as it would go. Shutting down or repenting publicly and changing drastically was not an option for these, they had too much at stake.

"As long as the gospel is preached, who cares what methods we use?" is how they consoled themselves.

Some, were unaware that a 'coup' had taken place, and though they were owners of sites and stations, the employees/ moderators/public who loved mixture had taken over their platforms, without accountability and rendered the webmasters and owners of TV/radio stations/print media etc., as mere puppet heads of such platforms, which they had once hoped would be for airing the truth. Such media-platform owners would occasionally rise up, like a drunken man in a stupor, speak or point to some truth but then soon be pushed back into the corner by the public 'demand' for mixture.

I saw mixture mixture mixture.

Strangely, these who promoted mixture became set in their ways and rather wasted precious time and resources warning against those who spoke and aired the truth. I saw that this they did out of jealousy and insecurity.

WHO'S MAD?
THE VOICE OF FESTUS

Listening, reading, viewing American media was soon becoming a pass-time for the 'insane'.

The right to Freedom of speech was being mutilated beyond recognition. The government, the people, the church had so scrambled the truth. I saw in a vision flash, that truth like a ball of wool, had been so unraveled, and knotted that it was no more useful, due to what looked like innumerable knots (which was lies).

Insane policies, laws, doctrines all had a well-established media-platforms to be aired from.

Wheresoever I looked at media I saw insanity woven into the news / views / opinions / reports / science.

Nations all over the world were rushing to look like America. All the modern world that was aping America was beginning to look like Universal Studios. Fake sets, fake homes, fake relationships.

Insanity insanity insanity.

The increasing sin in the land had so affected the minds of some people, in the church and in the nation, and world wide, I saw that with increasing sin, mental illnesses/disorders were increasing. (The Lord reminded me, within the vision, of the occasions I almost acted on information given by those I later realized were suffering from mental illnesses. Only His Grace Kept me from making a fool of myself)

I understood that world over people were acting on instigations and incitements of the suspicions / news / views / conspiracy theories of some of those who actually were mentally ill but the world mistook them for sane. Many playing the game of 'prophet profit' were basing their 'prophecies' on such hearsay.

Truth lovers in America found themselves surrounded in this environment of mountains of lies multiplying at an alarming rate, and certain news and views and opinions and reports of certain key/ powerful persons whose minds were bordering on insanity.

The Lord equipped truth lovers in America, and also world wide, with wisdom and right doctrine, so that they could bring timely correction to those who were going astray from following lies and liars. For this purpose, the Lord Had Equipped them to tear down and build anew on right and sound doctrines / truth. But many were in no mood for tearing down their long held structures, nor were they ready for the truth, rather they turned on those who spoke the truth.

These truth lovers heard against themselves the cry of those such as Festus, who said to Paul:

Acts 26:24... "And as he thus spake for himself, Festus said with a loud voice, Paul thou art besides thyself; much learning doth make thee mad."

The question in the coming times, in America and world over would be, "Who's mad?"

THE REMNANT WILL AIR THE TRUTH

I saw that the remnant in America understood the damage that the 'American gospel' had caused around the world. I saw that in small ways and sometimes in a big way, through prophecies, teachings, radio, and via every manner of media, spoken strongly and in no uncertain terms against the 'export of the American gospel'.

I saw that the Lord had already Sent some from other nations to America, and these too were Raiders of the Airways, for they relentlessly aired the truth.

VISION FLASH: RAIN AND ROCKET

In this vision-flash, I saw that those among the remnant, who had chosen any means of media to air the true, uncompromising Word of God, had been as rain-drops on a hot desert land. All they seemed to receive back was a vapor from the hot sandy ground.

Nonetheless in obedience they had stayed the course, though often they had asked the Lord, "What's the use, Lord, is ANYBODY listening? Does anyone care? Am I the only one left in this land? Who is interested in the truth?

And like Elijah, the Lord Had Shown them over time, there were others, who had not bowed their knee to Baal.

These had often wanted to give up but the Grace of God Kept them airing the truth.

Now I saw that from being rain drops in a desert land, suddenly their ministries / work of speaking the truth, challenging the false and lies, took off as rockets.

They saw unprecedented success.

I saw that these Raiders of the Airways, in America, who had used even the smallest means available to them to air the message of truth, saw unprecedented growth. I saw such as these prospering in their work through every means of media, be it newspapers, drama, T.V., Cinema, Radio, etc.

I saw vast avenues of media become available miraculously to the Raiders of the Airways. Many progressed suddenly from standing on a soap box, in a park and delivering their message of truth, to Radio, T.V., Cinema, and other forms of media from which they could reach a wider audience. I saw varied media avenues, now in the hands of the Raiders of the Airways.

I saw hidden talents in many come to the fore. These God-Given talents were 'aired'. Whilst some present day writers faded away, those who loved the truth and were not afraid to air it, found a God-ordained 'spot' to 'air' the truth from. I also saw messages of truth that came through drama, cinema, T.V., music, prospering.

PUT RIGHT AMERICA, PUT RIGHT

I think, around the early months of 2007, I had heard a word for the Body of Christ. 'Put right, put right, put right'.

I now heard it again in late 2007. This time it was ' Put right America, put right'.

I understood now within the context of all that I had seen and heard in my spirit, that the remnant who had been a lonely voice, in 'Desert America', would now be further equipped with powerful teachings and resources and they would go around the world and very specially to those nations that had been poisoned by the 'American gospel' and preach to them the true message of salvation.

I saw these remnant few wondering about who would listen to them, when in America, they received a deaf ear from most. The Lord Assured them, that their ONLY task was to put right, to go to the nations, warn about the 'American gospel ' and the dangers of believing and living it.

The remnant few were not expected to CONVINCE the nations, just tell the nations the truth, and if the hearers did not believe, and still chose to continue in the American gospel, then it would be UPON THEIR OWN HEADS, and they could not say that they were not warned. The Lord would Bring these nations to account.

I saw that: EVERY MANNER OF MEDIA WAS BEING USED TO 'PUT RIGHT' THE WRONG /FALSE TEACHINGS.

Whilst the truth lovers from America, aired or some personally delivered the true gospel message to the world, and warned against the filth that America was exporting, I saw the Lord also alerting such truth lovers of re-packaged messages of the false gospel RETURNING to America, via these very nations.

I saw that there were true and false preachers in all nations. I saw that though the Lord was Sending out many preachers from the world over (including India), to speak the truth to

America, there was a warning that there were some false preachers, from nations such as India, Australia, U.K., Canada, Singapore, Argentina, etc, who were bringing back to America, a re-packaged message which was really the same old false gospel, that had once been preached to them from America, but with new packaging.

I also saw that now the truth lovers had to be careful, to warn America of such imports of re-packaged messages.

In another vision flash, I had seen those like Zacchaeus, eager to make restitution, eager to put right, to give back to those they had cheated or deceived.

WHERE WOULD THE RESOURCES FOR THE REMNANT COME FROM?

I saw that God was Stirring the hearts of the wise craftsmen to work and stirring the hearts of the people to give sacrificially and abundantly. Whilst the mammonites in America wore Rolex watches, and wore flashy clothes, I saw that these Raiders of the Airways were simply but smartly dressed.

I saw men wearing simple clothes such as jeans and a T-shirt, in charge of vast resources.

I saw that these Raiders of the Airways, either traveled physically or their messages reached the far corners of the earth via media.

I saw as the Raiders of the Airways had a mission to air the truth, so there were people whose hearts were stirred in a mission to support this truth with unprecedented generosity.

I saw that the donors and the recipients did the work of the Lord joyfully. I understood within the vision that this would grow.

GOD WOULD NEVER DO THAT!

All over America, rose voices to refute that which the true prophets and servants of God, preached. "God would never do that", "God would never do that", " God would never do that", I heard this coming from every direction in America.

People who knew not the requirements of God and lived in sin and filth, seemed to 'know', what God would not do.

Such as these had refused to believe God's prophets and servants and had instead persecuted and reviled them. As Israel, in Eze 21:21 did not believe 'false divinations such as the looking at the liver' as a word from God, now God would convey to them prophetic words through means that would defy and challenge their 'sensibilities.'

DO NOT BE NAIVE, BEWARE HEROD

I saw the Herods in America, inquiring about the birth of new ministries, pretending to look interested as if they intended to help/support it. But really they wanted to kill it.

I understood within the vision, that wisdom and discernment and recognition of the Herods in America, helped the Raiders of the Airways, from seeking undue publicity or undue attention. They preferred to grow without the public gaze being upon them.

The Lord Had already Spoken to the raiders of the airways to be wise, as persecutions were coming.

Matthew 10:16... "Behold, I send you forth as sheep in the midst of wolves: be ye therefore wise as serpents, and harmless as doves."

I saw that like the wise men, when these broadcasters of the truth discerned the plans of the Herods, they departed into their own country another way.

[Source – S. Jha – tentsofissachar.wordpress.com]

I hope and pray that the above vision comes true in the very near future. As stated earlier, the sheer scope of the spiritual sickness and corruption that have been spread around the world via modern media is staggering to contemplate. And the false doctrines that have taken hold in the church have become so ingrained across entire regions and continents that it is going to take an enormous miracle even to make a dent in them.

But we live in momentous times. And I believe when God moves on all this, His enemies will be helpless to stop it. A great shaking and clean-out of the church lies directly ahead.

CHAPTER EIGHT

HALLMARKS OF THE REVOLUTION

So what exactly will the characteristics of this coming move of God be? What will be its main themes and teachings – designed to restore us back to full New Testament Christianity? Below we outline roughly a dozen of these hallmarks – things that God has highlighted again and again as being vital to the coming move of God:

A YOUTH REVIVAL

Some of the most powerful prophecies I have read state that this will be a "youth" revival as well as a great Reformation. But for that to happen, today's "entertain them at all costs" approach to youth ministry would have to be utterly overthrown. We must do away with "entertain, entertain, entertain." Instead the youth will have to be shown a cause worth dying for.

No doubt, "all ages" will be involved in the coming move of God. It is never confined to just the young. But I believe thousands of youth – from University all the way down to school-age – will play a vital part in this revival from the beginning.

To the Christian young people I say: The call of God is upon you – a call to cleanse your hands and purify your hearts – and to lead your entire generation to do the same. Only you can respond to this calling at this moment. Only you can say "Yes" to the revival that Jesus so badly wants to bring. If you do not rise up, then likely no-one else will. If you do not respond, this moment can be lost. Will you answer your calling? Will you respond to God?

I am convinced the Lord wants to raise up an army of young "Philips" in this generation. They will heal the sick and cast out demons. They will baptize and care for the poor. They will speak piercing truth – a message of deep repentance and heart-holiness. They will glorify Jesus – not themselves. They will have no interest in building their own kingdoms, taking on titles, or putting on a show. They will be humble servants of the Most High God – a glorious army for Jesus. And they will go forth, "conquering and to conquer," cleansing the land of defilement in His name.

Regarding healings and miracles, Jesus said, ***"These signs shall follow them that believe"*** (Mk 16:17). And the Scripture states that His followers ***"went forth, and preached everywhere, the Lord working with them, and confirming the word with signs following"*** (Mk 16:20). The coming move of God is to have both the "word and the Spirit joined". It will have piercing, anointed preaching, accompanied by the kind of "signs following" that we see in Bible days. Nothing less will do.

LEAVING THE CATHEDRAL

As we have seen, a "cathedral" mentality has been at the center of Christian practice ever since the dark ages (but not in the beginning). It is so ingrained today that we hardly even recognize it or the harm it is doing. Of course, it is not just church buildings that are the problem – though our focus on these is certainly an issue. It is actually the entire mentality of locking Christianity away behind four walls – a place where the 'respectable' people feel welcome while the unkempt sinners shy away. The very ones we are called to reach are the least likely to attend. The world is no longer hearing our message.

The Bride is going to "leave the cathedral" in the coming revival – both figuratively and literally. God is going to bring His people out from all these man-made trappings and obstacles. The common people will see God's power and hear His message once again. And Christianity itself is going to be unshackled from any structures or methods that have kept it boxed-in for so many centuries.

NEW MUSIC

When the church lives its life out before the world (as it should) there will come a great change in everything it does – including its music. A passive, insipid, "indoor" church produces music that is vastly different from the street-music of a 'warrior' church living out where the people are. This has actually happened in several revival movements down through history. They took their message outside the old structures and suddenly their music changed.

This is why three great men of God – Martin Luther, John Wesley and William Booth – were all credited with saying, **"Why should the devil have all the best music?"** In each case, they felt led to take the most popular drinking songs of the day and change the words to make them Christian songs. You can imagine the outrage and opposition this caused in religious circles! How dare they use the devil's music in this way?

But these men knew exactly what they were doing. They believed that ultimately, God owns all the music. And since they were trying to reach the "common people" for Jesus, a change in their music had to be made. And thus their message spread much further than ever before.

I believe something like this is going to happen again in the coming revival. But as always, it is likely to be highly controversial when it does. The heart and the message of the music is what matters, and this must always remain pure.

FULL BODY MINISTRY

Training and equipping literally every Christian to be a "minister" is going to be a big part of the coming move of God. Even very young Christians will be trained how to move in the authority of Jesus, how to lay hands on the sick and see them healed, how to baptize, how to give their testimony, how to move in the gifts of the Spirit, etc.

As stated earlier, the days of the "one man band" are over. The days of raising up the entire body to do the work of the ministry are here. We all know the Great Commission given by Jesus: *"Go therefore and make disciples"* (Mt 28:19).

A true disciple "takes up the cross" to follow Christ. A true disciple lives every moment with Jesus at the center of their lives. They are totally surrendered to God. His will is uppermost in everything they do. And more and more they are becoming like Him. That is their aim. Just like the first disciples, their goal is to become like Christ – in word and deed, in purity and power, in love and miracles – everything. They are His "imitators" – His 'apprentices'. And they aim to have the same impact for God that the early disciples had.

CONVICTION OF SIN

As Frank Bartleman of the famous 'Azusa Street' revival wrote: **"I received from God early in 1905 the following keynote to revival: 'The depth of revival will be determined exactly by the depth of the spirit of repentance.' And this will obtain for all people, at all times."** Amen! The whole of revival history shouts loud agreement with Bartleman's statement.

Another Pentecostal pioneer, A.G. Osterberg wrote, **"The Azusa revival began where every revival should rightly begin – in repentant tears. It began in tears, it lived on tears, and when** the tears ended the Azusa revival ended." This is why revival preaching has always been so heart-searching – so focused on "Sin, righteousness and judgment." It has always aimed to "cut people to the heart" – to convict them deeply of their sin.

As the leader of the 1904 Welsh Revival, Evan Roberts proclaimed: **"First, is there any sin in your past with which you have not honestly dealt, not confessed to God? On your knees at once. Your past must be put away and cleansed. Second, is there anything in your life that is doubtful – anything you cannot decide whether it is good or evil? Away with it. There must not be a trace of a cloud between you and God. Have you forgiven everybody – EVERYBODY? If not, don't expect forgiveness for your sins..."**

When Jonathan Edwards preached his famous sermon, *Sinners in the Hands of an Angry God,* the record states that **"The assembly appeared bowed with an awful conviction of their sin and danger. There was such a breathing of distress and weeping that the preacher was obliged to speak to the people and desire silence that he might be heard."**

Such preaching – anointed by the Spirit – always produces abundant good fruit in the lives of the hearers. It is the lack of this conviction and deep repentance in the modern church that has produced such lukewarmness in nation after nation across the globe.

PROPER CONVERSION

As discussed earlier, for years we have gone around the world telling people to "repeat this little prayer" or "ask Jesus into their heart" in order to be saved or converted. But we have known for a long time that the results of this 'convenient' little method are often sadly lacking. The raw statistics certainly bear this out.

In his excellent book, **Hell's Best Kept Secret,** Ray Comfort makes the point that modern evangelism is often so tragically ineffective that it boasts only a 20 percent holding rate. He also quotes one evangelistic campaign involving 178 churches in which only three percent of the converts remained. **"How effective are our present-day evangelical methods,"** he asks, **"when they create eighty backsliders for every one hundred 'decisions for Jesus'? Some are even less effective than that,"** he continues. **"One recent campaign reported having a 92 percent backsliding rate!"** (*Hell's Best-Kept Secret,* Page 1).

In the coming revival, a lot of these modern "methods" are going to be discarded in favor of truly biblical practices. The way of conversion is going to go back to the "full foundation" that the apostles laid in the book of Acts. For every new convert, it will be expected that there is deep conviction of sin and true repentance. Then they will be taken and baptized right away – without delay. And hands will also be laid on them for the infilling of the Holy Spirit (and speaking in 'tongues').

All these things will be expected to happen on day one. New converts will take off like a rocket ship – fully repented, baptized and filled with the Holy Spirit from the very first hour. It will be the "full foundation" of Hebrews 6:1-2 (which we see used throughout the New Testament), not some cheap "rote prayer" method that produces lukewarm results.

THE POWER OF BAPTISM

Today's church often treats water baptism merely as some kind of "symbol" or ceremony. The deeper meaning and the true power of baptism that we see in the Bible is utterly lost. Yet in Romans chapter 6 we read the following:

"Do you not know that as many of us as were baptized into Christ Jesus were baptized into His death? Therefore we were buried with Him through baptism into death" (Rom 6:3-4).

Please note that Paul refers to baptism as a "death and burial" with Christ. One thing we have found very powerful is to tell people to take this literally – by FAITH. That baptism really is a burial of their old life. That the 'old man' truly is being cut off, killed and buried with Jesus. That baptism is exactly what the Bible says it is – and by faith they need to take hold of it so their entire past can be left behind.

When people are baptized in faith this way, the whole thing becomes much more meaningful and much more powerful. They truly experience the cutting-off of their old life. And it is not even uncommon for some to be delivered of demons as they are being baptized. That is how life-changing the whole experience can be. No wonder the apostles always baptized people right away!

I believe this lost power of baptism is another thing that is going to be fully restored in the coming move of God. Everything is going back to the New Testament – how it was originally designed to be.

PRAYING IN TONGUES

The coming revivalists will be all about being filled to overflowing with the Holy Spirit – and getting others filled also. The book of Acts tells us: *"And they were all filled with the Holy Spirit and began to speak with other tongues, as the Spirit gave them utterance"* (Acts 2:4). We need to realize that this is a baptism of holiness. After all, it is God's "Holy" Spirit filling our lives. His holiness, His power, His love, His victory over sin. That is why it is so important.

Tongues is also vital for prayer. Paul said, *"I speak in tongues more than you all"* (1 Cor 14:18), so he obviously prayed in tongues a lot. I often tell people to make it a habit to pray in tongues quietly wherever they are – doing housework, reading, working, driving. Pray in tongues the whole time. It is a most effective form of prayer – and powerful ministries have risen up just through praying this way every day. It is one of the great secrets to moving in God's authority and power.

Pray in tongues every moment and make it a habit. This is something that can cause your ministry to take off in ways it has never taken off before.

MINISTRY TO THE POOR

It is very clear from Scripture that Jesus' ministry was mainly aimed at the needy and hungry ones of His day. Jesus Himself said: *"The Spirit of the Lord is upon Me, because He has anointed Me to preach the gospel to the poor"* (Luke 4:18). He also described His ministry in this way: *"The blind see and the lame walk; the lepers are cleansed and the deaf hear; the dead are raised up and the poor have the gospel preached to them"* (Matt 11:5).

As disciples, we are called to continue Jesus' ministry in the earth. His mission is now our mission. All the way through the New Testament we see this emphasis on the poor and needy. And this is also where we can expect the greatest miracles. For the poor of the earth tend to have a simple faith. They tend to be spiritually hungry, and since they have little access to healthcare, their needs are that much greater. God will often meet such ones at their point of need. And thus the healings multiply.

"The poor have the gospel preached to them." This will be said of the coming move of God also. Recovering this sense of mission to the orphans and widows, the needy and the hungry ones, is vitally important to the recovery of full New Testament Christianity in our day.

MAMMON DETHRONED

Since the "mammonite" gospel has become so entrenched around the globe, a deep cleansing is required. Just think for a moment of all the verses about this in the New Testament alone:

"Come now, you rich, weep and howl for your miseries that are coming upon you! Your riches are corrupted, and your garments are moth-eaten. Your gold and silver are corroded, and their corrosion will be a witness against you and will eat your flesh like fire" (James 5:1-3).

"No servant can serve two masters... You cannot serve God and mammon" (Luke 16:13).

"But those who desire to be rich fall into temptation and a snare... For the love of money is a root of all kinds of evil, for which some have strayed from the faith in their greediness" (1 Tim 6:9-10).

"But woe to you who are rich, for you have received your consolation" (Luke 6:24).

There are many other passages that say similar things. I am convinced that the coming revival in places like Africa and Latin America will drive corruption and the love of money out of the church. (For judgment begins "at the house of God"). Only after the church is cleansed can we expect society to be cleansed also. It is the corruption in the pulpit that first has to go.

AN ARMY WILL RISE

There is a revival of righteousness coming to the nations of the earth – a mighty revival of repentance and "holiness unto the Lord". God will use the lowly and the disrespected to humble the mighty and the proud. Healings and miracles will occur at the hands of the very young. Out of the mouth of babes will come piercing truth that will cause even kings to tremble. We live in the most momentous of days. Only those who are prepared and praying will be part of this revival from the beginning. Tell me, friend – is that you?

Truly, "many that are first shall be last, and many that are last shall be first" in this move of God. Those involved will be a company of the humblest kind – tried, broken, trained and tested – who will emerge from the deserts as if from nowhere, full of the glory of God, hearts washed white as snow, with a mighty word in their mouths.

We are headed for the most tumultuous – but glorious – of times. I pray that everyone who reads this will be among those who not only "survive", but who actually 'thrive' in these days – to the glory of God the Father. May the Lamb who was slain truly receive the reward of His suffering.

Amen.

VISIT OUR WEBSITE –

www.revivalschool.com

APPENDIX A

= SHOCKING BIBLE STUDY =

THE LOST FOUNDATIONS

(1) Welcome to a Bible Study that may surprise and even shock you! (As it does with a lot of people). If you want to get the most out of it, please write your answers to each question below.

(2) As you read each of the Bible passages, please answer each question-

(a) Please READ Heb 6:1-2. Then write out the "six foundations" below (numbering them)-

ANSWER -

How important do you think these six things are?

ANSWER -

What words does verse 1 use to describe these six things?

ANSWER -

Before we continue, let us talk briefly about Repentance and Faith, since these are such crucial things in any true conversion. What is Repentance? It is a "turning away" from sin involving 'Godly sorrow', confession to God and a real heart-change. What is genuine Faith? It is a simple childlike belief and trust in Christ's righteousness - not our own - to justify us before God and save us.

Both of these things are clearly totally essential to salvation. But what about the other Foundations?

(b) One major thing that we are looking at in this section is whether or not the early church used the "sinner's prayer" to lead people to the Lord - or whether they used the FOUNDATIONS instead. What exactly did the apostles tell people to do to become truly converted? Did they ever use the "sinner's prayer"? If not, what did they use instead?

The book of Acts is probably the best place to start in answering these questions, as it is the only book where we actually see thousands upon thousands of people becoming converted.

READ Acts 2:37-38. What were the 3 things that Peter told the people to DO in response to the gospel? (Please number them)-

ANSWER -

Please read on through verse 41. Do we see any signs of the people saying a "sinner's prayer" or giving their "heart to the Lord" like we do today?

ANSWER -

How soon did they baptize them?

ANSWER -

(c) READ Acts 8:12-17. Again, in this passage, do we see people "asking Jesus into their heart" or "praying a little prayer" like we do today?

ANSWER -

Again, there seemed to be 3 important elements in their response to the gospel. What were these 3 things?

ANSWER -

How soon did they baptize them?

ANSWER –

What was the "laying on of hands" used for?

ANSWER –

(d) READ Acts 10:44-48. Is the pattern here similar to what we have just seen in the other passages? In what way?

ANSWER -

Do you think these people may have already been godly, holiness-seeking people - even before Peter preached to them? Give reasons for your answer.

ANSWER -

How did the onlookers know that these people were filled with the Holy Spirit?

ANSWER -

Was it "optional" for them to be baptized?

ANSWER -

(e) READ Acts 11:15-18 and compare it with Acts 10:44-48 and also Acts 2:4. Does it seem that being "filled with", 'baptized with', or "receiving" the Holy Spirit may all refer to the same experience? Quote Scripture to back up your answer.

ANSWER -

Also, in light of these passages, do you think that the Spirit "coming upon" or "falling upon" someone is generally referring to this same type of experience?

ANSWER -

(f) READ Acts 19:1-6. Do we see any signs of people saying a "sinner's prayer" or giving their "heart to the Lord" in this passage?

ANSWER -

Do you think these people had already repented - even before Paul preached to them? Give reasons for your answer.

ANSWER -

Write out the "pattern" of what happened to these people when they responded to the gospel preached by Paul.

ANSWER -

Is it basically the same pattern that we have been seeing in the other passages?

ANSWER -

How could Paul tell that they had been filled with the Holy Spirit?

ANSWER -

(g) The conversion of Saul (who later became Paul) is recounted in Acts 9 and also Acts 22. Please READ Acts 9:1-18. Do we see (1) Repentance, (2) Baptism and (3) Receiving the Holy Spirit in this passage?

ANSWER -

In this and other passages, did it seem to matter too much what ORDER baptism or the infilling of the Spirit occurred? Give more than one scriptural example as proof of your answer.

ANSWER -

(h) Let us look again at how soon people were baptized in the Bible. Did they have to wait 6 weeks, 6 months - or was it immediate? Please READ Acts 16:25-33. At roughly what time of day were the Jailer and his family baptized?

ANSWER -

Does the above passage give the impression that baptism is very important? In what way?

ANSWER -

Please READ Acts 8:35-38. Do you think Philip spoke about baptism when he was preaching the gospel to the Eunuch? How can you tell?

ANSWER -

Based on these passages, and all that we have seen, how soon do you think we should baptize people?

ANSWER -

We have now looked at virtually EVERY conversion that is detailed in the entire book of Acts. At any time did we see anyone "asking Jesus into their heart" or repeating a "sinner's prayer" in order to become a Christian?

ANSWER -

After all that we have seen, do you think that when people ask "What should we do?", then our best answer might be the same as Peter's on the Day of Pentecost? Please WRITE OUT Acts 2:38 below-

ANSWER -

(i) Let us now seek to answer this question: Is water baptism mostly just an outward "SYMBOL" - or is there something powerful happening SPIRITUALLY in baptism?

Please READ Rom 6:3-8. According to this passage, what happens to our "old life" through baptism?

ANSWER -

Please READ Col 2:11-12. According to this passage, what is happening inside of us when we are baptized?

ANSWER -

Please describe what the term "circumcision of the heart" means to you-

ANSWER -

Regarding the practice of 'sprinkling' little infants, the Greek word "baptizo" means to "dip or immerse" - not sprinkle - and the two passages we have just read describe baptism as a "burial". Therefore baptism surely has to be by "full immersion" under the water. Do you agree?

ANSWER -

And anyway, little infants are not old enough to "believe" the gospel first. Please READ Mark 16:15-16. Can a little baby "believe"? And therefore, according to this passage, should they be baptized?

ANSWER -

OBJECTIONS TO THE TEACHINGS ABOVE

There are several objections that people often raise when they hear this teaching. Often they are trying to defend the idea that all we need to do is "pray a little prayer" to become a true 'Bible Christian'. They do not want to admit that the scriptural pattern is (1) Repentance, (2) Baptism, and (3) Receiving the Holy Spirit. Below are some of the main objections that people seem to raise-

(a) "What about the Thief on the cross?" - OUR ANSWER: We believe in "death-bed" repentance, and this is certainly an example of that. But it should also be noted that this took place BEFORE the New Covenant truly began - before Jesus died and rose again - and before the Spirit was given at Pentecost. Therefore it is not a very good example for us to copy if we want to experience a full New Testament conversion.

(b) What about Romans 10 - which is so often quoted as a kind-of "formula" for becoming a Christian? - OUR ANSWER: Please READ Rom 10:9-13. The first question we must ask is- Is this passage meant to be an actual 'formula' for salvation? Is that the actual purpose of it? Please give your opinion.

ANSWER -

Secondly, it is a wonderful passage about FAITH - a very important topic. But who is it written to - believers or unbelievers? Who is likely to be reading the book of Romans? Might Rom 10 perhaps be written differently if it really was a "salvation formula" being written to unbelievers?

ANSWER -

Thirdly, when we look at the OVERWHELMING evidence on the side of "Repentance, Baptism & Receiving the Spirit" - and we look at the fact that we cannot find anyone in the whole Book of Acts simply "praying a prayer" for salvation - shouldn't we go with the overwhelming Bible way? Surely we have to look at what the "weight" of Scripture teaches - and go with that? Isn't this what we should always do in these situations - go with the overwhelming "weight" of Scripture? Please give your opinion.

ANSWER -

Fourthly, Rom 10 says that "Whosoever calls on the name of the Lord shall be saved". But perhaps we should ask ourselves- "When did Paul himself first 'call on the name of the Lord'?" When did this moment occur for him? Please READ Acts 22:16 and write below the actual words that Ananias spoke to him-

ANSWER -

As we can see from the above passage, the moment when Paul first "called on the name of the Lord" was actually IN BAPTISM. Do you find this significant?

ANSWER -

Ultimately, I do not find Rom 10 to be conclusive proof against our teachings - or for the idea of a "sinner's prayer". It does not make sense to take that meaning from it when the whole rest of the New Testament teaches something different.

(c) Many people ask, "What about the old Revivalists and Reformers from past centuries? The Christianity of their time did not involve Baptism by Immersion or being filled with the Holy Spirit. What about these heroes of old?"

OUR ANSWER: I actually believe that God has slowly been restoring His truths to the church bit by bit over the centuries, since the Great Reformation. If you look at history you will see that it started with "Justification by Faith" in the 1500's, then the "New Birth" and Sanctification, then Baptism by Immersion, then healing, then Baptism of the Spirit with 'tongues', etc, until today we have the opportunity to fully enter into virtually everything that the early church entered into - and powerful Spirit-filled Revivals are happening around the globe.

The church has come full circle in many ways, but still I feel we need one last Great Reformation to fully restore all that was lost. It has taken a very long time for the church to emerge out of the dark ages, and there have been many "heroes" along the way. To me, men like Luther, Wesley, Whitefield, Finney, etc, are a great inspiration - and I write about them and preach about them all the time. But yes - they lived in an era when Christianity seemingly had less light than she does today. Thus I believe all the people of those times will be judged by the light that they walked in. It is as simple as that. I do not condemn them at all - in fact I admire many of those old preachers and learn as much from them as I can.

(d) "Do you believe in Baptismal Regeneration?" - OUR ANSWER: No! We certainly do NOT believe in Baptismal Regeneration - which is basically an old Catholic doctrine. All we are saying is simply that the Bible way of becoming converted seems to be through Faith, Repentance, Baptism and Receiving the Holy Spirit. It is quite different from what we have been taught to preach today, and I believe we are short-changing a lot of people. Don't you think this has to be one of the most important topics that Christians today could possibly discuss? Please comment.

ANSWER -

(e) "Couldn't this be seen as a kind-of Salvation by works?" - OUR ANSWER: Absolutely not! Where are the "works"? Is Faith a work? Is Repentance a 'work'? Is water-baptism a work? (It is quick, it happens only once, and the person does not even do it to themselves - so how can they be "working"?) Is baptism with the Holy Spirit a 'work'? In my opinion, none of these things are remotely like 'works' at all. Where is the "working" going on? Please give your opinion.

ANSWER -

(b) Have you ever heard the verse Rev 3:20 "Behold I stand at the door and knock..." being used out of context to get people to 'ask Jesus into their heart'? Does it surprise you how utterly out-of-context it is?

ANSWER -

(c) When Andrew Strom commented that he now baptizes "In the name of the Father, the Son & the Holy Spirit - in the name of Jesus Christ" - what was his reason for adding "In the name of Jesus Christ" onto the end?

ANSWER -

(4) Please look up the following Bible passages and answer the questions-

(a) READ 1 Cor 10:1-2. This Scripture is using a "type and shadow" from the Old Testament to make a point about the New. If the Israelites were "baptized into Moses" in the 'cloud and in the sea' then what do you believe would be the New Testament equivalent?

ANSWER -

(b) Please READ Gal 3:27. Do you think there is a connection between this verse and the passage that we just read (1 Cor 10:1-2)? If so, what?

ANSWER -

(b) Please READ 1 Peter 3:20-21. Again, there is a type and shadow from the Old Testament being used here - this time Noah and the Ark. Peter says that Noah's family was "saved through water". What does he say is the New Testament equivalent of this?

ANSWER -

(c) Please READ Titus 3:5-6 and compare it with John 3:5. There may or may not be a connection between these two passages. Do you think so, and if so, what is it?

ANSWER -

(d) Please READ Matt 28:19. In light of this verse, do you think it is possible to "make disciples" without baptizing them? Quote the Scripture to back up your answer.

ANSWER -

(e) We ourselves tend to hold to the classic Pentecostal position regarding "tongues" - that generally they are the 'initial evidence' of getting filled with the Holy Spirit that we expect to see. Please WRITE OUT the following verses-

Acts 2:4

ANSWER -

Acts 10:45-46

ANSWER -

Acts 19:6

ANSWER -

Acts 8:17-18

ANSWER -

Mark 16:17

ANSWER -

1 Cor 14:18

ANSWER -

Of course, this baptism of the Holy Spirit is a baptism of Holiness and Power and Love and Victory over sin - which are the big important things that we expect to see in a person's life after this experience. But we regard tongues as an important "initial evidence" of receiving the Holy Spirit. -And vital for ongoing prayer also. Paul said "I speak in tongues more than you all." So he obviously prayed in tongues a lot. Shouldn't we do likewise?

ANSWER -

(f) OBJECTIONS TO 'TONGUES'

Some people believe that the gifts of the Spirit are not for today at all. This seems rather a ridiculous argument to us, but we cannot go into it here. The objection that we find most common is that many believe tongues is only for "some" believers - and yet we believe that God desires ALL His children to have such a 'prayer-language'.

The passage that seems to confuse people most is found in 1 Corinthians. Please READ 1 Cor 12:29-30. Because this passage asks "Are all apostles, are all prophets... Do all speak in tongues?" (to which the obvious answer is "No"), people are left thinking that tongues is only for 'some'. But what they fail to notice is that this passage is speaking about "ministry gifts" in the church. The whole passage is listing 'ministry-offices' that some are called to. And one of these is to "speak out publicly" in tongues during a church meeting - which must always have interpretation. Only certain people are called to do this. That is the point Paul is making.

They have a special anointing to use tongues as a public ministry - which is not for everyone. But certainly he is not talking about the private "prayer language" that we believe Scripture shows is available to every believer. If you read the entire chapters 1 Cor 12 - 14 with this in mind, we believe it will clear up a lot of confusion. There are two different types of tongues. One is for public ministry (which must be interpreted) and the other is for private use in personal prayer (-available to everyone). Does this explanation make sense to you?

ANSWER -

(5) Having studied this topic so thoroughly, do you now have the desire to go out and see people Repent, be Baptized, and be Filled with the Holy Spirit? Is that the type of conversion you want to see happening from now on?

ANSWER -

(6) HOMEWORK: Please go to at least 3 of your friends and acquaintances. Gently and lovingly share these Scriptures with them and make sure that they have been baptized and filled with the Holy Spirit. (Please be gentle!)

(7) FURTHER HOMEWORK: For further study on this topic you can simply look up every Scripture on Baptism and also the Holy Spirit - as well as the other Foundations - in the whole New Testament. Please use an "exhaustive" concordance if you wish to do such a study.

VISIT OUR WEBSITE –

www.revivalschool.com